DISCOVERY
ALASKA TO HAWAII AND THE PACIFIC

DOCUMENTATION	
Name:	
Ship:	
Date of Voyage:	
Stateroom:	

For Ari:
Aloha from the Big Island!

J*** Louise
July 6, 2021

DISCOVERY
ALASKA TO HAWAII
AND THE PACIFIC

LOUISE RIOFRIO

For brothers and sisters in the Pacific, especially my friends in the Haida and Tlingit nations of Alaska.

Contents

INTRODUCTION	6
PROLOGUE: ISLANDS	12
ALASKA: GREAT LAND	40
HAWAII: HOMELAND	108
TAHITI: DISTANT LAND	186
AOTEAROA: NEW ZEALAND	228
I'A: GALAXY	320
REFERENCES:	331
ABOUT THE AUTHOR	337

INTRODUCTION

Aloha and Gunalcheesh!

Aloha means both hello and goodbye in Hawaii, while Gunalcheessh means "thank you" in the language of Alaska's Tlingit.

You are about to discover the Pacific, either on a ship or through the pages of this book. You will be introduced to the land, the wildlife and the people. If you are a native and think you have heard everything, you will experience an even bigger pleasure. You are reading a story almost no one knows, how our Pacific Ocean was first explored. This story has been hidden in the mists of history, but has been uncovered for your enjoyment. All the peoples of the Pacific should read this story with great pride.

In the Pacific we use phonetic vowels. Translated roughly into English phonemes:

    A is pronounced *ah*.

    E is pronounced *eh*.

    I is pronounced *ee*.

    O is pronounced *oh*.

    U is pronounced *oo*.

The name of *Aotearoa* is pronounced: "Ah-oh te-ah ro-ah".

The "t" and "k" sounds are nearly interchangeable. The Hawaiian *kapu* is the Tahitian *tapu*.

Many Polynesian words contain the apostrophe or glottal stop. This indicates that two adjoining vowels are pronounced as separate syllables. The name of Hawaii may also be spelled "Hawai'i," but I use the common spelling. The similar names Hawai'iki and Hawai'iloa are spelled with the apostrophe.

Some words are only roughly translated into English letters, because early Polynesians lacked a written language. The word and place name Kona has other spellings, but I use the popular one. We will see that Northwest American dialects contain extremely similar words.

Words have power, and even proper spelling is important. The seagoing people of Vancouver Island are properly called the Nuu-chah-nulth, a name they officially adopted in 1978.

Though the Haida and Tlingit have been historically considered as separate peoples, I often refer to them in one breath. We will see that they share common mothers. The naming of tribes is often arbitrary, sometimes imposed by outside colonizers.

Though European explorers arrive late in this story, some of their names appear before their chapter arrives. In particular, the names of Captain James Cook, Captain George Vancouver, and Thor Heyerdahl often appear in the Pacific.

A word about titles: The commander of a ship is always called Captain, regardless of pay grade. Captain Cook began his *Endeavour* voyage as a new Lieutenant, but was still Captain of the ship. The Polynesians he encountered regarded Cook as a great chief. Among the people of Vancouver Island, a sea captain is also a chief. Cook's predecessor Nuu-o-Kahinali'i is called Chief Nuu to distinguish him from the later Lua Nuu.

Many tribe members suffer from lack of direction or low self-esteem. I hope that this book instills a sense of pride, for you are part of a great voyaging people. This also applies to the tribe that works in Space Centers. You are also part of a voyaging tradition.

We discover new things every day, and this second printing of the book contains much new information and photos taken across the Pacific,

Marcel Proust said that the true voyage of discovery consists not to visit lands but seeing with new eyes. I hope this book leads you to see your home with new eyes, and see the wonders our ancestors saw.

PROLOGUE

ISLANDS

June 14, 2008 AD

The sky rained in the morning, but the launch continued.

The canoe was the first built by the Tao of Dongching Village in eight years. Following tradition the canoe was decorated in colours of red, white, and black. Chevron patterns represented ocean waves. A stick figure holding curlicues represented the first man. A circular symbol at the bow represented both an eye and the power of Light.

Tao villagers attended the launch wearing traditional costume. A man's status among the Tao depends on his ability as a fisherman, and normally a boat is built by one family. The skills to build a canoe have faded over time, so this time the whole village contributed to the launch. Families who were sometimes rivals made critical contributions.

As the ceremony began, villagers congratulated the boat owners by rubbing noses together. Sixty men wearing loincloths chanted together as they carried the canoe toward the shore. In unison they lifted it up and down with their arms moving as one. With a great shove, the canoe ascended into the air.

That same day *Discovery* returned from the sky.

Following tradition, the Space Shuttle was decorated in white and black. While in orbit she had delivered a new part of the Space Station. The Kibo module was built in Japan, a relatively short voyage from Orchid Island. After crossing the Pacific on June 14, Discovery landed at Merritt Island. We know this island as Kennedy Space Center.

I believe that one Light can overcome darkness. You may have heard of me as the Scientist who predicted that THE SPEED OF LIGHT changes with time, a *Discovery* that changes everything. I stopped in Taiwan on the way to give a talk at an International Astronomical Union meeting on the island of Bali.[i] In the words of Harvard University's John Huchra, it was "a delightful talk by Louise Riofrio on how a non-standard cosmology with a varying speed-of-light might reproduced the high-redshift supernova Hubble diagram". I solved one of the darkest mysteries of science.

Returning to Taiwan I lingered longer, enjoying the island's unique culture. Taipei is a very modern and technologically advanced city, at that time site of the world's tallest building. Taiwan is also home to many indigenous tribes, who arrived thousands of years before later immigrants. Of the 23 million people in Taiwan barely 400,000 aboriginals are left. I considered staying in Taiwan, for teaching work there is plentiful.

Graduate school advisers angrily told me that I had no future in science, but I enjoyed an honest living as a model and actress. Since watching spacecraft lift off on television, I was inspired to explore the universe. Working on a film set is a lot of waiting, but the waiting paid off. Starting in 2008 I've worked as a Scientist at NASA Johnson Space Center in Houston.

Studying the Moon and planets has been a dream come true. I was entrusted to perform experiments with priceless Apollo Moon samples that had been untouched for 40 years. In my spare time I used the Moon to measure whether the speed of light is changing. The job of Scientist has taken me to many exciting places, up to the summit of Mauna Kea in Hawaii. From the islands of Taiwan, Kennedy Space Center is 12 time zones away, the far side of the world.

On a planet of oceans, the Pacific is greatest. The name means "peaceful". Viewed from space, the blue Pacific appears to cover half the globe. The name of Earth is a misnomer, because ¾ of the planet is ocean. The Pacific's many millions of square miles are dotted by thousands of islands. They are tiny dots compared to the vastness of the ocean. This story travels to some of those islands.

The question of our beginnings, like the origin of the Universe, is common among people everywhere. We learn in school about the civilizations of Egypt and Sumeria. Today we know that cities just as ancient were built on islands like Cyprus or Bahrain. To a sailor in the sea the sight of an island is a welcome relief. For seagoing people an island was a refuge, a source of resources, and a natural fortress. Even today the islands of Taiwan are protected from larger neighbours by the sea. America is virtually an island, "from sea to shining sea".

My ancestors were sailors, used to living surrounded by the sea. *Polynesian* is a European-derived term meaning "of many lands". For us the Pacific is simply *Moana*, the Ocean, a part of our existence. Captain Cook marveled at how far we had spread. Everywhere his ships explored in the Pacific, he found people already there. The "Polynesian Triangle" is anchored by today's New Zealand and Easter Island in the South, with Tahiti roughly in the centre and Hawaii at the apex. All these islands were settled centuries before Captain Cook. Where Pacific peoples originated is one of the great mysteries.

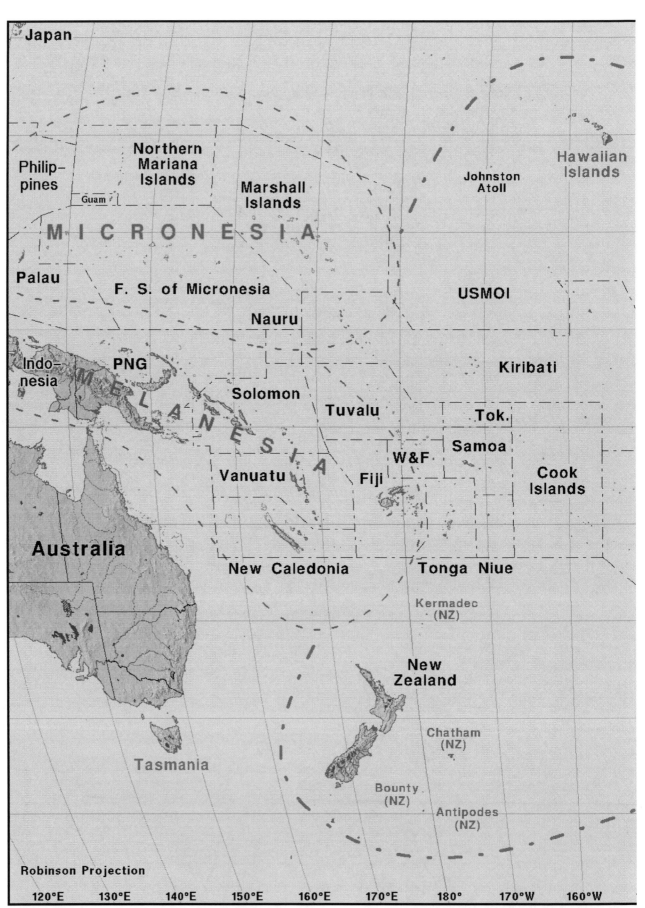

POLYNESIA is one of the three major regions of Ocean
Tuvalu, Tokelau, Cook Islands, Kiribati, USM

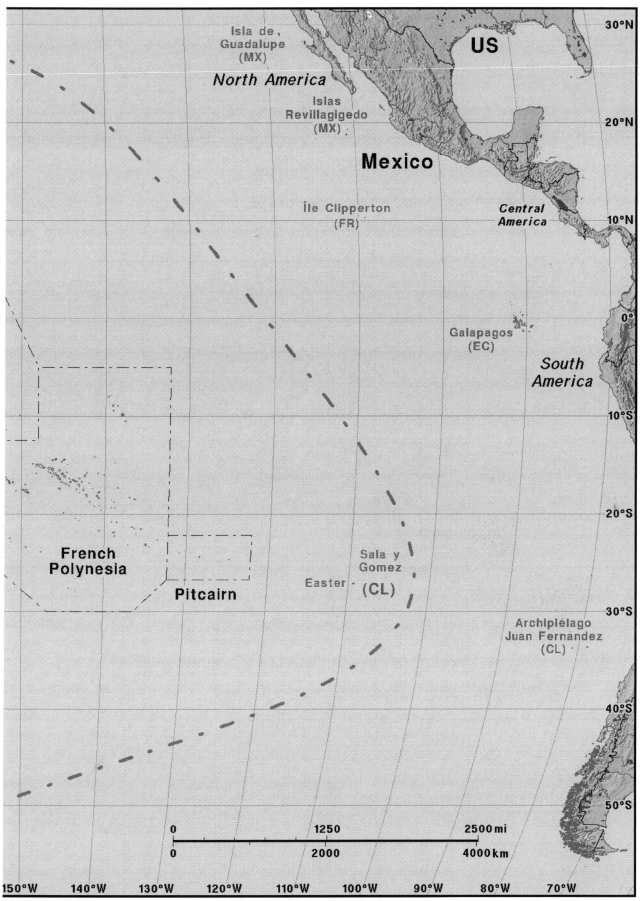

...ia with similar ethnicity. It includes New Zealand, Tonga, Samoa, Niue, ...OI, French Polynesia, Pitcairn, Hawaiian Islands and more; >1000 in all.

How the Pacific people voyaged is one of today's discoveries. Today we know that they were among history's great navigators. Many centuries before the Europeans, Pacific wayfinders explored Earth's greatest ocean without compass or chronometer. They steered by wind, stars, and currents. They sensed the presence of land by patterns in the waves. The migration of birds and sea life led them to new islands. In this way the rough Pacific was settled.

The Disney movie *Moana* brought a story of Pacific navigation to many fans. I am a fan of the movie, as I have often dreamed of battling darkness and faraway places. Part of me wished to explore like the ancestors. Across the Pacific, a history of voyaging is a source of great pride.

A child's first learning comes from the lessons of her family. Since ancient peoples had no written language, they relied upon oral tradition. Knowledge of history, stars and navigation was passed in spoken form across many generations. Storytellers had amazing memories--some oral histories took days to recite. Pacific navigators knew the names of hundreds of stars. Family genealogies stretch back over many generations. Our origins and voyages are part of this oral history.

The Maori people of today's New Zealand know of a homeland called Hawa'iki, somewhere to the northeast, either an island or a group of islands including one with that name.[ii] In Tahiti the legendary homeland is called Hawai'i and lies to the north. Northeast of the Maori and north of Tahiti are the Hawaiian Islands. The legends of Hawa'iki and Hawai'i do not exist in Hawaii, suggesting that they are all the same place.

Our Hawaiian Islands are the world's most isolated, more than a thousand miles from any other inhabited land. Though Ferdinand Magellan crossed the Pacific in 1521 AD, not until 1778 did Captain Cook find Hawaii for Europeans. Even Cook's Polynesian guides had forgotten that our Islands existed. Hawaii's remoteness caused resistance to the idea that Polynesians came from here, but Hawaiians must have come from somewhere.

We have more than one story of the first Hawaiians. One of the best-known traditions is of Hawai'iloa, a great fisherman who was at sea for months at a time. He followed the seven stars of the Pleiades constellation westward to discover Hawaii.[iii] He returned home in a canoe filled with vegetables and fish to tell what he had found. To get close to the original story, we can defer to a chief.

High Chief Solomon L.K. Peleioholani

(1844-1916) was descended from all Hawaii's royal bloodlines. His great grandfather distinguished himself fighting alongside Kamehameha the Great. Starting from his childhood in Hamakua, near Waipio Valley on the Big Island, Solomon Peleioholani learned to memorize Hawaiian oral history. As a High Chief, he had access to history that was secret from others. I read his story of the first Hawaiians from the archives of Honolulu's Bishop Museum.

"The ancestors of the Hawaiian race came, not from the islands of the South Pacific—for the immigrants from that direction were late arrivals there—but from the northern direction (welau lani), that is, from the land of Kalonakikeke, now known as Alaska.

"Kalonakiko-ke (Mr. Alaska) and Hoomoe-a-pule (Woman of Dreams), his wife, arrived at Ka-houpo-o-kane before it was disrupted by the flood which occurred in the reign of Kahiko-Luamea.

"According to this tradition it was at the land of Kalonakikeke that the floating log of wood named *Konikonihia*, which was carried away by the flood that occurred in Ka-houpo-o-kane, the island continent, came to rest.

"The legend relating this great deluge is recorded in an old prayer, supposed by some to be the same prayer offered to Kane by Nuu, who with his wife, their three sons with their wives, were saved on a canoe called Ka-waa-halau-alii-o-ka-moku (the royal canoe of the continent) when it rested upon Mauna Kea, on the island of Hawaii."

History of Hookumu-ka-lani Hookumu-ka-honua

Nuu-o-Kahinali'i, (Nuu of the Flood) appears in Hawaiian genealogy as son of Lalo-o-Kona (father) and Ka-Mole-Aniana, was married to Lili-Noe and had three sons. According to genealogy, Nuu is separated by 101 generations from Kalakaua, the last King of Hawaii.[iv] King Kalakaua, who was born in 1836 AD, also recounted the stories of Nuu and Hawai'iloa sailing from the East[v]. Assuming an average generation of 21 years, Nuu was born around 280 BC.

This oral history of has the hazy quality of a tale told many times. Words and places may have been lost or confused over the centuries, but it is a first clue to our beginnings. Kane is the chief Hawaiian god. Ka-Houpo-o-Kane, "bosom of Kane," is the place of origin of Hawaiian people. Today we can search for our origins from a genetic trail.

Our life is spread by the double helix of the DNA molecule. It carries the genetic record of our ancestors, which it reproduces by unfurling and then replicating itself. Mitochondrial DNA resides in the membrane of a cell but not in the nucleus. It survives in our egg cells, but sperm cells lose this DNA when they fertilise egg cells. As a result mitochondrial

DNA is passed down through generations via the female line.

Humans gain protection from disease through molecules called antigens, which trigger an immune response. These antigens are passed on through generations, helping ensure survival against disease. Polynesians share common Human Leukocyte Antigens (HLA) with Native Americans.[vi,vii] Tragically both populations were devastated by diseases like smallpox, from which they had no immunity. An unusual gene called HLA B48 is found in Hawaiians, America, and especially in the islands of Taiwan.

A Professor from Oxford University writes that our ancestors can be arranged by clans. 95 percent of Europeans belong to one of seven clans, each clan descended from one woman. These clan mothers needed to have at least two daughters to have started one of the clans that continues today. The clan of Ina, also known as Haplogroup B, is most closely related to the Pacific peoples. This clan has DNA sequences numbered 189 217 and 189 217 261.

The woman called Ina was born somewhere in the Western Pacific. Ina's descendants are also found in South America, Central America, Vancouver Island, and sporadically in Southeast Alaska.[viii] Her DNA is not found in Siberia or central Alaska, so it must have spread by sea. DNA sampling is not complete for Alaska, because smallpox and measles devastated many native villages--some communities lost 90% of their population. Studies show that the clan of Ina originated in the region near Taiwan.[ix] Another study from 2005, involving 640 people from nine Taiwanese tribes, found mutations shared only with Polynesians.[x]

An Alishan Tribal House at Taiwan Indigenous People's Cultural Park, Pingtung County, looks almost exactly like an Alaskan tribal house, down to the totem poles. Lake Alishan was a fishing ground for Taiwanese aboriginals. The modern architects who completed this cultural park may have been influenced by Alaska, but totem poles have long been carved in Taiwan. Though commonly associated with America poles have independently risen in Korea, New Guinea, New Zealand and Hokkaido.

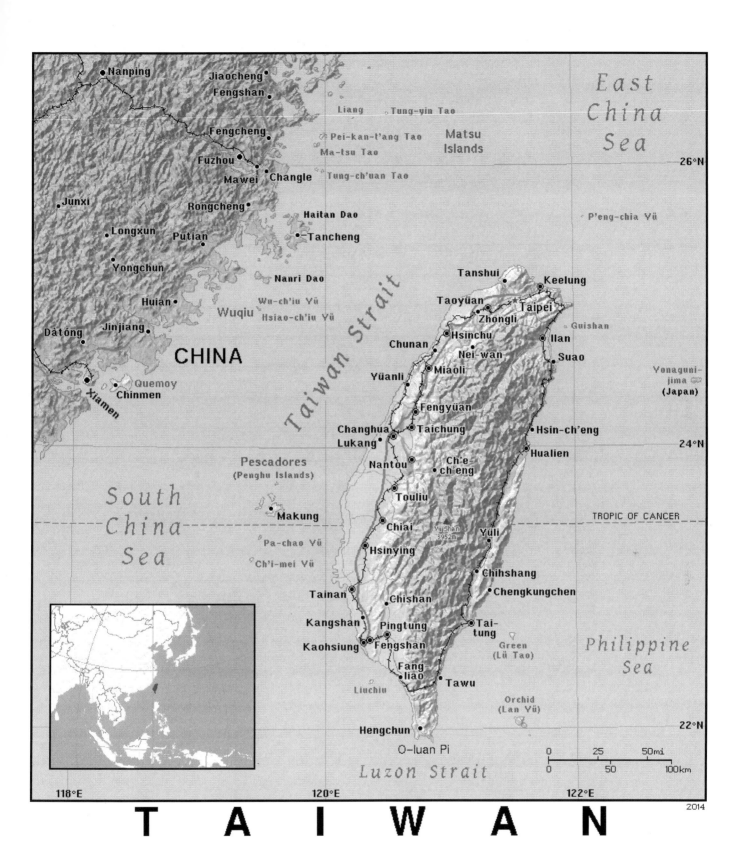

The Sheng Ye Museum in Taipei, not far from the National Palace Museum, sports a Taiwanese totem pole reproduced in concrete. The museum also proudly displays a canoe launched by the Tao of Orchid Island.

紅　頭　嶼（臺東廳）

Orchid Island, also known as Lan Yu, rose from the sea southeast of Taiwan in the fire of volcanic eruption. The name Tao means "the people" as it does in the Philippines and Guam. The native Tao, who have roots in the Philippines, are the only surviving seagoing tribe among Taiwan's aboriginals. Tao culture has always been linked with the sea and the Flying Fish. When a son of the Tao tribe is born, his family plants a tree. When the son is old enough to fish, the family will build him a canoe from this tree. Today the population of the Tao numbers barely 4,000.

From March to June is the **Flying Fish** Festival, when the Kuroshio Current brings fish from the Pacific. The flying fish is an amusing and tasty creature. 40 different species of Flying Fish swim in the waters surrounding Orchid Island. During the Festival, the Tao dress in traditional costume and chant for the return of the Flying Fish. As we saw in 2008, launch of a fishing canoe is a proud ritual. A Tao canoe and totem pole travelled to Pasadena as China Airlines' prizewinning float in the 2016 Rose Parade!

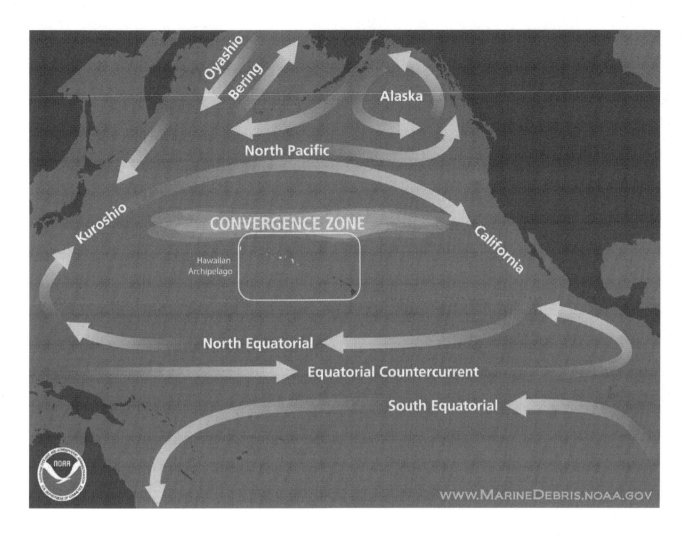

The Kuroshio Current is called "the black tide". It merges with the eastward currents to form part of the North Pacific gyre, a huge clockwise circulation spanning the width of the Ocean between Alaska and the equator. The black tide carries far more water than the Mississippi, Amazon, or any inland river. Earth's rotation, the Sun's warming, and Coriolis forces drive these immense currents. The westward Equatorial Current makes direct travel by sea from Asia to the Polynesian islands difficult, but sailing to Alaska is going with the flow.

"One if by land, two if by sea," says the American poem about Paul Revere. The first part of Hawaiian oral history, an epic sea voyage from Asia to Alaska, is today supported by science. In 1979 AD Dr. Knut Fladmark proposed a Pacific Coast Migration theory. Most archeologists of the time thought that America's first people walked via an ice-free corridor in today's Bering Strait. Fladmark pointed out that receding ice would have left few plants or animals for humans to live on, and thought that the ocean was a better route.[xi] Fladmark's theory was ignored for many years, but recent studies show convincingly that America's first people came not by land but by sea.[xii]

Archeologists have found that humans lived in Monte Verde, Chile by 13,000 BC. Other sites show that humans lived in America when ice made the land route impassable. Their DNA, known as Haplogroups A, C, and D, is a trail leading from Asia across the sea to Alaska and beyond. Hawaiian oral history leads to the route of the first Americans!

According to this history, Mr. Alaska arrived at Ka-Houpo-o-Kane, the island continent, before a great flood. Around 4000 BC the Early Holocene period ended. Sea levels rose with the melting of polar icecaps, possibly causing floods. Many cultures' legends, like the biblical Noah, contain stories of rising waters. This period may also have seen floods of people. Immigration from the mainland would have put pressure on Taiwanese islanders to find new homes across the sea.

Legendary Mr. Alaska would have arrived from a land of seafarers. Today the Tao are Taiwan's only indigenous tribe to maintain the tradition. In recent years, an "Out of Taiwan" theory has proposed that voyagers from this region settled the Pacific starting about 4000 BC. Today's genetic evidence supports this migration.[xiii] One interpretation says that Mr. Alaska and Woman of Dreams had already been to Alaska, and were chiefs there. To follow Konikonihia, their floating log of wood, we must voyage the Ocean.

I have had the opportunity to travel the path of great discoverers, an adventure beyond description. I have travelled on aircraft, small canoes and giant ships. I have met with native people, birds, whales, and unusual forms of life. They are guides, for the paths of wildlife tell the paths of people.

Discovery in the Pacific is history's greatest story of exploration, 6000 years in the making! Oral history tells of an ancient sea odyssey to Alaska, and a later voyage to Hawaii. Genetic evidence supports the story, and points to a beginning near Taiwan. On Orchid Island the seagoing Tao still launch canoes to follow the Kuroshio current and the Flying Fish. Modern science has learned of a Pacific Coast Migration, the first route to the island called America. This is a mystery with clues spread across half the Earth. Space, time and Pacific currents lead a voyager to a Great Land.

ALASKA

GREAT LAND

August 25, 2016 AD

The morning fog hung over Glacier Bay, painting the world in brushstrokes of grey. The cries of birds filled the air. First the drums were heard signaling an arrival, then the rhythm of singing voices. From the fog the canoes appeared. Their bows were decorated in red and black like the crew's oars. The rowers had trained for weeks, even painting their own oars. They rowed and sang to the same rhythm that their ancestors knew centuries before. On the shore, hundreds of people had gathered for this arrival. For one brief day, the Tlingit returned to Glacier Bay.

Since entering Glacier Bay by sea that August, I have returned to stay near here. The study of stars and navigation has taken me on planes and ships around the Pacific, and led to Alaska. Birds and whales provide clues to the Polynesian mystery. If you travel through Alaska, you will also find *Discovery's* trail.

Hawaiians have a memory of *Wao Lani,* a place from where our first descendants originated, a place of cold. In *Wao Lani* white clouds form leis around steep mountains, a sight rarely seen in Hawaii. Many times I have seen cloud leis around Alaska's steep mountains. Goddesses of snow and mist, Poliahu and Lili-noe, are said to dwell on volcanic peaks. Lili-noe is reincarnation of the wife who voyaged with Chief Nuu. A third goddess, Kalaua-kolea, is associated with a bird that flies to Hawaii. Ku of the canoe and *adze*, a legendary builder is reputed to live hidden in the forest, where a woman called Lea picks trees to turn into canoes. It is a place of quiet, respect and reverence. Hawaiian memories of *Wao Lani* are an excellent description of Alaska.

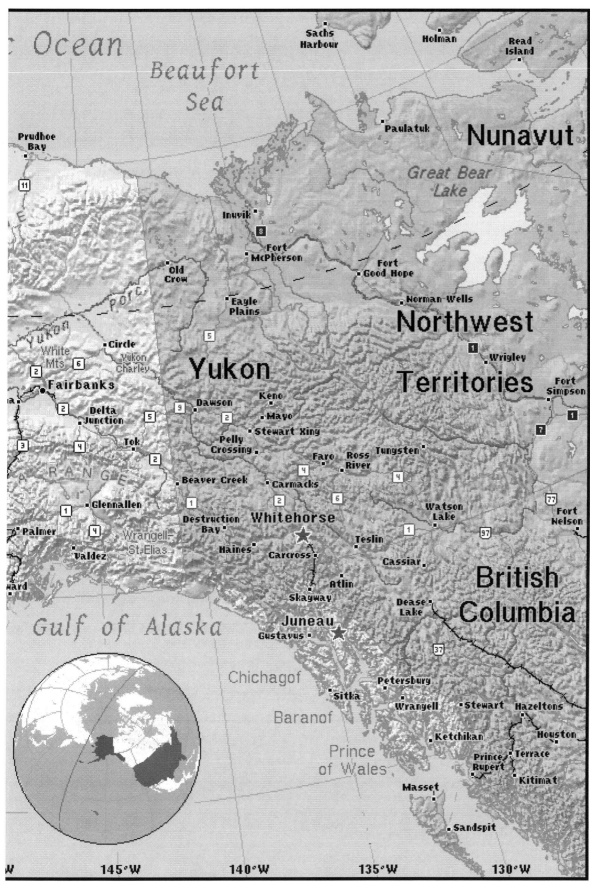

SKA

The origin of the name Alaska is foggy, but thought to be from a word meaning "Great Land". Alaska is, second to outer space, America's last frontier. It was also gateway of the first Americans. The Inuit live to the North near the Bering Strait. The Aleuts settled the islands stretching like pearls from Asia. Native peoples of the southeast include the Tlingit, Haida, and Tsimshian. Alaska still contains vast stretches of open space to explore.

At 4:30 AM on the first of May, while I was camping by the water, the forest and I woke to an earthquake! My ear and body already to the ground, I felt the Earth move in waves passing through and past my body, then reverberating back twice. Intimately I felt the magnitude 6.2 quake and its 6:20 AM aftershock reflect back and forth. Later in May Bogoslof Volcano in the Aleutians erupted, sending clouds of ash 30,000 feet into the air.

We are on the Rim of Fire. Beneath the ocean is the Pacific Plate, an enormous tectonic structure that is continually in motion. Movements of plates and continents, the creation of the land we live on, is driven by Earth's internal heat. The edges of the Pacific Plate collide with continental plates and are pushed beneath the surface. Many volcanoes, some of which are always active, surround the Pacific.

Migration to Alaska has been going on for a long time, over 200 million years. The Pacific Plate in its movement carries great *terranes* of land. Southeast Alaska sits atop the Alexander Terrane, a rock canoe that drifted from across the sea before crashing into North America. Evidence for this collision comes from minerals, fossils, and magnetic rock. Later the Chugach Terrane crashed into Alaska, joining the pileup. These impacts created four great mountain ranges alongside each other, separated by three underground fault systems. The Denali Fault System contains three river valleys, including the Chilkat River Valley north of Glacier Bay. Fossils of tropical ferns millions of years old have been found in Alaska, early migrants from across the Pacific.

Southeast Alaska is, like Hawaii, a place of islands. The Inside Passage from Glacier Bay to Puget Sound contains many hundreds of islands. Sailing north or south involves crossing Dixon Entrance and Queen Charlotte Sound, bays wide open to the Pacific. Glacier Bay and even Alaska's capitol Juneau are virtual islands, inaccessible by land. The only way to travel this archipelago is by sea.

Glacier Bay is in the Fairweather Range, among the world's tallest coastal mountains. Mount Fairweather rises 15,325 feet, higher above sea level than Mauna Kea. This perpetually snow-covered peak dominates views both from the ocean and from Glacier Bay, and is easily spotted by mariners. The National Park and Preserve is as big as Connecticut and nearly empty of people. The length of Glacier Bay uncovered by ice is longer than San Francisco Bay. This is one of the most spectacular places on Earth. More than a dozen giant glaciers feed into the Bay. Every day we can see huge chunks break off, or *calve*, into the water with a thundering crash. The many inlets fill with ice particles large and small.

With few humans, Glacier Bay is ruled by wildlife of air, land and water. The sky is patrolled by bald eagles and other raptors. The forests surrounding Glacier Bay are green and thick with life.

On land we can see moose, black bears, brown bears, wolves, mountain goats, and some very large porcupines. The frigid waters are home to playful otters, sea lions, orcas, and in Summer the humpback whales. Camping by the water at night, I've heard the Call of the Wild.

Southeast Alaska is a land of plenty, long the home of hunters and gatherers. The native people have never needed to farm for food. The forests grow berries which are enjoyed by birds, bears and humans. The seas grow fish, octopus and the Alaskan King Crab. The rivers are full of salmon. Each salmon, after living in the sea, must return to its place of birth to spawn and then die. During the months of Summer bears and eagles feast on the salmon.

Around the time hunter-gatherers first voyaged to America they brought a valuable friend. Approximately 13,000 BC dogs were first domesticated in Asia and possibly in Europe. The first American dogs were descended from Siberian breeds like the Husky. Today's Alaskan dogs are mostly Spitz breeds, like the Malamute. Alaskan Huskies are a mix of various breeds. They all have big smiles, warm coats and small upright ears.

In the forests surrounding Glacier Bay, rocks and trees alike are coloured with the green of **lichen**. Lichen is mix of fungus and algae, one of the first life forms to appear after the glaciers receded. It only grows in places where the air is 98% free of pollutants. Clouds that form in the cool air float just a few hundred feet above sea level, girdling the mountainsides in necklaces of white.

Beneath the surface of Glacier Bay is another forest, made of **kelp**. Kelp plants are a form of algae that anchors to the sea floor. They have no roots, but draw nutrients directly from the seawater. Sea urchins feed on the kelp, and otters feast on the urchins. Herring and mackerel spawn in the kelp beds, attracting other fish and even whales. Kelp forests grow just beneath the surface, through which light streams as if through a cathedral. Diving through a kelp forest is a heavenly experience.

For sea voyagers, the kelp forest can be a seafood buffet. One can even anchor a canoe to it. Since kelp forests grow from Asia to Mexico, in recent years a "Kelp Highway Hypothesis" has suggested that early voyagers used them as stepping stones to cross the Pacific. These voyages began around 14,000 BC, before humans were supposedly walking across the Bering Strait. The sea route from the Taiwan region to Alaska passes through many kelp forests, a trail of bread crumbs. On this highway there were many Mr. Alaskas, including the first Americans.[xiv]

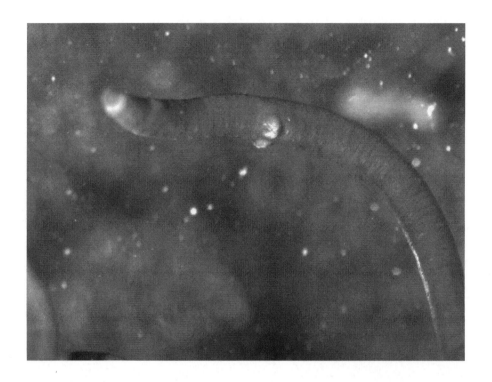

The glacial ice is home to a unique form of life, the **Ice Worms.** They were discovered living within Muir Glacier in 1887. These amazing creatures thrive in temperatures near the freezing point of water. They feed on algae and microscopic life—a single glacier can contain billions of them. Ice Worms live only in Alaska and the Pacific Northwest, but are a type of life we may someday find beneath the surface of Mars or icy moons. Even in this extreme environment, life has burrowed a way in.

Raven, a playful and talkative friend, is omnipresent in Alaska. He greets us with his cackling nearly every day. Ravens are very smart—they can play games, solve puzzles, and even outwit humans. A Raven will open a clamshell by leaving it in the middle of a road, knowing that a car will come by to crack it. One new study claims that Ravens can learn and plan for the future.[xv]

For the Northwest peoples Raven is a trickster and demigod, able to change shape at will. In mythology Raven brought men Light. In most of these stories, Raven is born human and later transforms into a bird. One story often told in central Alaska is about Raven and a whale. The whale tale must have arrived by sea, for whales don't go to central Alaska! Stories of Raven are centred in the Kamchatka Peninsula. Raven's trickster tales travelled the ocean with the first Americans.

The Eagle has landed! In Alaska I've been looking after a Bald Eagle named Lady Baltimore. The Eagle is symbol of the U.S. and queen of birds. They live primarily on fish; a rich source of protein. Once endangered, the Eagle is returning in 49 states, nesting as far as Houston and Florida. They build their gigantic nests in high places close to lakes or streams. Of the 70,000 bald eagles in the wild more than 30,000 make their home in Alaska. They enjoy the clean air and abundance of fish.

Eagles can also be aids to navigators. They station themselves on trees and points of land, announcing their presence with distinctive cries. A canoeist on the foggiest day can find the shore by listening for the eagles. An eagle's flight path indicates the direction to land, and can show the way to fish. Each winter when the salmon streams freeze, thousands of eagles fly to a hidden destination, which Tlingit discovered by following the eagles.

All Tlingit tribes are divided into two clan crests, *moieties* of Raven or Eagle. If your mother is Raven you are Raven. Upon marrying, Raven must choose a spouse from Eagle, and vice versa. According to the Tlingit, this custom creates balance. Presciently it preserves the mitochondrial DNA of clans, which passes through the female line. The custom encourages marriages and alliances between different tribes and clans. Other tribes have moieties of Wolf, Bear, Orca and other familiar animals.

The name Tlingit (pronounced Klink-it) translates to "people of the tides". They fished and hunted in Glacier Bay for centuries, careful stewards of its resources. The canoes arrived on that foggy August day for the dedication of a new tribal house. The house was built with modern materials from a traditional plan.

The words the Tlingit sang upon their arrival may sound familiar to *Moana* fans. "Hu-way, hu-way"! is a Tlingit cry.

Tlingit oral history tells of great cold and starvation, a "Year of Two Winters" when Summer never came. People of the tides rowed south across Icy Strait to found the town of Huna, which thrives today. Scientists studying tree rings in Glacier Bay have found a period of little or no growth during 1754 and 1755 AD. This coincided with eruptions of Taal Volcano in the Philippines in 1754 and of Iceland's Katla Volcano in 1755. These events darkened skies worldwide. Tlingit oral history is supported by today's science.[xvi]

US Secretary of State William Seward bought Alaska from the Czar of Russia in 1867. He travelled here with scientist George Hamilton in 1869 to observe an eclipse of the Sun. He had heard of the Whale House of the Chilkat, a fabled tribal house with carvings centuries old. The local Tlingit were very impressed when the eclipse occurred on August 8, exactly as the scientist had predicted. They invited Seward and Hamilton to enter the Whale House, and gave them a map of Southeast Alaska. The Tlingit map showed lands that even Captain Vancouver had not found, including a land route into North America.

When Vancouver sailed here in 1794, he could not find Glacier Bay because it was choked with ice. Even the Gastineau Channel to Juneau was impassable. 85 years later Naturalist **John Muir** was drawn here by stories of glaciers. In California's Yosemite Valley Muir had become convinced that glaciers could carve Earth's surface, but the geology community ignored him. Just as some claimed that THE SPEED OF LIGHT is fixed, rocky heads of 1879 insisted that Earth's continents were inviolable. How could mere ice carve solid rock?

With a Tlingit crew and a local missionary, Muir ventured into the mists on a small canoe. Sitka Charlie, the youngest of the crew, had childhood memories of hunting with his Tlingit father in a bay of ice. When fog and rain made them stop, Muir climbed a mountain in the cold to look around. Before he reached 1000 feet, the rain ceased and the clouds lifted like a curtain.

Alone on a mountaintop, John Muir found himself surrounded by gigantic glaciers stretching as far as his eyes could see. He saw what Earth looked like during an ice age. Vast perpetually frozen ice fields fed slow-moving rivers of white. The ice carried within it dark streaks of rock called *moraines*, which ground Earth's surface like sandpaper. What

Muir saw told him that stories of a Glacier Bay were true, and he was right about ice carving into Earth.[xvii]

On a later trip to a glacier Muir brought along a dog named **Stickeen.** The dog was Muir's enthusiastic companion during canoe voyages, the first to go ashore upon landing and the last to return. They became trapped on the wrong side of a crevasse, which both had to cross on a narrow bridge of ice. The adventure taught Muir and Stickeen new respect for each other.[xviii] Stickeen was one in a tradition of dogs in Alaska..

In the copilot's seat of a DeHavilland Twin Otter seaplane, I had an eagle's view of the glaciers. North of Glacier Bay is a field of ice flowing from the mountains. Behind the capitol Juneau is another enormous icefield, which feeds the Mendenhall and Taku Glaciers among others. Cold air flowing down from the glacier makes the town of Juneau a cool place.

In a Tlingit canoe I paddled to the face of a glacier. It is the one of the best upper-body workouts available! Glacial ice starts as the fall of white snowflakes on the mountainsides. Over centuries icefields thousands of feet deep have formed. Gravity crushes the snow into ice that ends its journey at the glacier face. Ice calving from the glacier face forms icebergs large and small. As our canoe drifted by a big iceberg, I reached out and touched its face.

Beneath this glacier I hiked into a cave of blue ice. Glaciers appear this colour for the same reason that Earth's sky is blue, the scattering of light. The ice made in a freezer is white from tiny cracks and imperfections. Glacial ice is crushed over centuries until no gaps or cracks remain. Longer wavelengths of light are absorbed, but the shorter wavelengths are scattered to colour the ice blue.

In Alaska we may see **Aurora Borealis**, the Northern Lights. They are the product of charged particles from the Sun cascading into Earth's magnetic field. The glowing curtains follow vertical field lines, circling the North Magnetic Pole. Simultaneously *Aurora Australis*, the Southern Lights are visible in their hemisphere. These twin poles of Earth's field are manifested in Light. The hidden source of the magnetic field puzzled even Albert Einstein, and is the subject for another book.

All things in nature, even THE SPEED OF LIGHT, change with time. As the Early Holocene period ended around 4000 BC, vast sheets of ice that had covered North America receded and the land filled with life. The rocky land was first painted by the green of lichen, and in time, the forests grew. The greening took centuries, so humans walking across the Bering Strait would have very little to live on. In Glacier Bay, we see signs of change and migration

Life has returned to Glacier Bay since the Little Ice Age and its Year of Two Winters. The Tlingit who left for Huna are still not allowed to return. The National Park and Preserve now occupies the land. The new Tribal House is a small gesture toward a hopeful return. On May 20, 2017 the Tlingit erected two new totem poles depicting Raven and Eagle.

A female humpback whale called **Snow** rests forever nearby. Using the marks on her tail, scientists have followed Snow since the 1970's. During 2001 she had a tragic collision with a cruise ship. After many months of work, Snow's remains were preserved for our learning. Her tragedy has contributed to science--we learned from Snow that humpbacks can live at least 96 years. The whales migrate to Glacier Bay every Summer. Like drummers on canoes, they announce their presence by singing or leaping out of the water. [xix]

Near Glacier Bay I photographed a pod of **Orca,** Killer Whales. The latter name originally meant "killer of whales," for they do not threaten humans. Orcas are among the most intelligent of sea creatures.

An Orca can easily defeat a Great White Shark. Orcas cooperate top herd fish together for feeding. They spend their lives in pods, which allow them to gang up on even bigger prey. In part because of the Orca danger, humpback whales give birth across the sea.

Walking along Glacier Bay's shore trail, I found a canoe on display. Native Alaskans built it in 1987 using traditional techniques, carving from a single log. Like our spacecraft, the canoe is one of the greatest expressions of a culture's technology. *Konikonihia*, the floating log of wood said to have carried Mr. Alaska and Woman of Dreams, would have been chosen and named in a ceremony even before being cut down. This log was carved and hollowed with a tool called an *adze*. It was shaped with steam, filled with water and hot rocks to bow its sides, and finished without nails. As on Orchid Island, every step of launching a canoe was an honoured ritual.

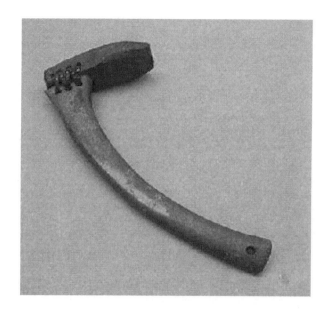

The **adze** is a popular tool across the ocean. It looks like an axe turned ninety degrees, or a chisel with a handle. Historic adze blades were carved from the hardest stone. While the lumberjack's axe is useful for cutting trees down, the adze is better for fine carving. It can turn logs into planks for building, or carve a log into a canoe. The adze would spread by canoe from Alaska across the Pacific.

Travel by canoe was a family affair bringing along spouses, children and even grandparents. Everyone to the smallest child helped in rowing and bailing. The position of steersman, guiding the craft with an oar, often belonged to women. In canoes like this, Alaskan families travelled to the Aleutian Islands, British Columbia and beyond. Today we can follow some of the voyages.

On May 15, I was accosted by three men carrying guns. The law could not help because remote Alaska has no law. I was left to live or die 12 miles outside the nearest town on a very cold night. I heard the eagles, and could find my way from their calls. A Tlingit woman whom I had befriended earlier gave me a lift into a town. With thanks to eagles and the Tlingit, I've explored many corners of the Great Land.

Cook Inlet

    I first flew over Alaska in a US Navy plane. On a clear day, we can see Denali all the way from Anchorage and Cook Inlet. Formerly called Mount McKinley, at 20,320 feet it is the tallest mountain in North or South America. On the shore of Cook Inlet in Resolution Park, Captain Cook commands the view. Possibly he is wondering how the Polynesians had spread across the Pacific. In 1779 he sailed into this inlet on his last voyage of discovery. His crew were the first Europeans to meet the peoples of Hawaii and British Columbia. Cook did not know that he was meeting keepers of the Pacific secret.

The first inhabitants of Anchorage were the Dena'ina, a name that also means "the people". They speak a Na-dene language similar to that of the Tlingit. Dena'ina tribes are also divided into two moieties. According to Dena'ina legend, Raven created two women who were mothers of these moieties, and in turn were ancestors of the various clans.[xx] Through this female line their mitochondrial DNA was spread. The Dena'ina, a seagoing people and the only central Alaskan tribe to live on the coast, arrived after 500 AD.

Joseph Greenberg, who was considered the great classifier of languages, thought that Na-dene languages descended from a mother tongue in Siberia.[xxi][xxii] His colleague Merritt Ruhlen thinks that Na-dene represented a migration from Asia to Alaska around 4000 BC. Ruhlen thinks that Na-dene speakers arrived in boats, landing in the islands called Haida Gwai'i. Greenberg's work was ridiculed for decades, but modern DNA proves a Pacific Coast Migration.[xxiii][xxiv][xxv]

The **Navajo**, America's second largest native tribe, and the Apache also speak a Na-dene language. Though the language of World War 2 Navajo code talkers was thought incomprehensible, the Tlingit can easily understand it. Tlingit also served as code talkers in that war; their brave service has been kept secret until recently. Linguist John Campbell concluded that the Na-dene languages of Alaska were related to Polynesian tongues.[xxvi]

The Navajo and Apache migrated to the Southwestern US from Alaska around 1400 AD. Hawaiians knew of a similar people they called the Na-Wao. The classic lines of an American Indian canoe, with double upturned ends, echo the Tao of Orchid Island. Alaska was origin of many native American tribes, who first arrived by sea.

When traveling down the Alaska Peninsula, we may see the **Pacific Golden Plover**. These little birds mate and nest in flat dry ground from late April to July. In early August the females take off across the sea, leaving the males to care for their newborn. Later in the month males also leave. After growing a few more weeks, the chicks take off in the same heading as their parents. The little Golden Plover is also a clue for navigators.

During 2016 archeologists digging in the Seward Peninsula, which juts into the Bering Strait, found a metal pieces and belt buckle with some of the leather still attached. The belt was dated to nearly 1000 years old. Metal found in a place with no mines is proof that native Alaskans traded with Asia.[xxvii]

Aleutian Islands

One stop for navigators was Sanak Island, which spreads from the peak of a volcano. Core samples show that the surrounding area was free of ice by 15,000 BC, offering a clear path for voyagers. Sanak Island is surrounded by kelp forests, which sustain a sea otter population that has attracted humans in boats.

Hawai'iloa, the fisherman said to have found the Hawaiian Islands, sailed from a "Sea of Kane". If he was at sea for months at a time, Hawai'iloa would have found no better fishing ground than the Bering Sea, which even today provides fish to millions.

THE SEA-OTTER FISHERY OF ALASKA.

Archeologists have found signs that Sanak Island was inhabited around 4000 BC, the time voyagers from the Taiwan area were reaching into the Pacific.[xxviii] In modern times, the island supported a fishery and a few houses, which are still intact. Today Sanak Island and its houses are deserted, but wild cattle still comb the beach feeding on kelp. The Aleutian Islands extend like steppingstones across the ocean. If Mr. Alaska and Woman of Dreams originated in Alaska, there must be another homeland here.

Some have suspected the connection between Alaska and Asia. Lieutenant George Emmons of the US Navy spent many years with the Tlingit, and noted how they resemble Asians in appearance. Charles Marius Barbeau, one of the founders of Canadian anthropology, did fieldwork across Canada. He proposed that people traveled from Asia to Alaska by sea, like the seagoing tribes that still exist today.[xxix] Today's Pacific Migration Theory supports these connections.

Thor Heyerdahl before *Kon-Tiki* lived during 1939-40 in British Columbia. He noted the many similarities between Northwest peoples and Polynesians. They both enjoy greeting by rubbing noses together. Place names like the Straits of *Tonga'as*, and the *Hakai'i* Channel sound Polynesian down to the glottal stop. Heyerdahl thought that the ancestors of Hawaiians paused in the Pacific Northwest. Their currents take us into Dixon Entrance and the homeland of the Haida.

Haida Gwai'i

The name of the Haida tribe also means "the people". Haida Gwai'i, once called the Queen Charlotte Islands, means "Homeland of the people" as does Hawaii and Hawai'iki.

The 138 islands were born, like Hawaii, in the fire of volcanic upheavals. At the northern tip of Haida Gwai'i we may hike to Tao Hill, a volcanic plug 2 million years old, rising above lava fields. The name is often misspelled "Tow" in maps, but Bill Reid and other Haida prefer "Tao Hill". The significance of this spelling is left to readers of the prologue. Nearby is a blowhole called "The Gun" where we can see water shooting into the air. Once this archipelago was called Xhaaidlagha Gwaayaai or "Islands at the edge of the world".

Its remote location led Haida Gwai'i to spawn unique species—some call it the Northern Galapagos. Here we can see the Sitka Deer and hear the Hairy Woodpecker knocking. We may also glimpse the Haida Gwai'i Black Bear, whose powerful jaws can crack shellfish. Though this homeland is remote, from its shore we can see the islands of Alaska.

Haida and Tlingit history begins here. They tell of a great flood, like that of the Hawaiian story. On Rose Spit, the hook of sand jutting into the sea past Tao Hill, Raven is said to have found the first men hidden within a clamshell. The talkative bird encouraged them to leave their shell and emerge into the world. Later Raven found the first women within another seashell. The sculpture by Haida artist Bill Reid was on Canada's 20-dollar bill.

From the Pacific, the eastward Kuroshio splits into the northward Alaska current and the southward California current. During Summer these rivers pass close to land at Rose Spit. At this natural hook, littered with driftwood, pieces of Asian bamboo and coconut have been found. In 1916 a fishing boat off Shimoda, Japan, was disabled in a storm and drifted powerless to Dixon Entrance in 24 days.[xxx] Ships caught in the currents could easily end up at Rose Spit.

Mr. Alaska, Woman of Dreams, and others on the voyage may have endured great hardship. The great circle route from Taiwan to Haida Gwai'i passes near 58 degrees North, latitude of the Aleutian

Islands. Solomon Peleioholani tells of them praying amid foaming, surging seas of Ha'aleiwawahilani, an arctic ocean. The voyagers would have endured storms and cold in an open boat. They may have run low on food, so that clams on a beach would be a welcome meal. Since Raven is omnipresent in the Northwest, he may indeed have found these First People chewing on a clamshell.

In another Haida story, a man and his wife were blown to sea by a north wind, and landed in a country where the people wore red coats. (Native Alaskans often wear red.) They stayed in a cave for four years, and were treated well until the natives told them it was time to leave. Guided by a seagull and two Orca, they came to Haida Gwai'i. There a war party from a hostile tribe killed the man, but the woman escaped to tell the tale.

Wracked by riptides and winds, Rose Spit was not a good place for seafarers to settle. They would have wanted a home sheltered from tides, a harbour for canoes. They would need a source of fresh water, secluded from hostile tribes. Raven's cackling encouraged these First People to explore their new world. Looking across the waters of Dixon Entrance, they would have seen Alaska.

Dall Island

A very old story among the Tlingit tells of some strange people who were swept from the western ocean and were first to reach the coast, settling on Alaska's Dall Island. Among them were two sisters who met and married men who had travelled down the rivers of North America. The younger sister and her family crossed to Haida Gwai'i and founded the Haida. The older sister remained in Alaska and became mother to the Tlingit.

Dall Island, nearly uninhabited, is seaward of Prince of Wales Island. On the west side of Dall Island is Gold Harbor, which opens to the Pacific and is surrounded by sheltering mountains. At the inner end of this fjord is a small beach, a perfect place to land canoes. Just 100 feet from the beach and a few feet above sea level is a cave of white marble.

This home was discovered in 1992 and named Kit'n'Caboodle Cave for its riches. In a time of cave dwellers, this was a marble palace. Near one of the four entrances, we heard the rushing of an underground stream. The floor of one room is covered in fish bones, the history of many seafood feasts. Other rooms contain a museum of remains-- deer, otter, even an eagle. Kit'n'Caboodle Cave was the home of early sisters, daughters of a mother who traveled the sea.

Shell *middens* are the remains of seafood meals. When someone from a seafaring culture finishes eating, her shells join the midden. Prehistoric middens can contain millions of shells. The shell beach you walk on may be the remains of someone's midden. Shell middens inside Kit'n'Caboodle Cave cave date from before 3500 B.C., the time Woman of Dreams would have arrived.[xxxi]

In Tlingit history one sister remained in Alaska. Based upon shared words and place names, at least one researcher has concluded that Tlingit ancestors once lived on the coast of Haida Gwai'i.[xxxii] The "people of the tides" travelled north and founded settlements across Alaska's islands. According to Emmons, one group of Tlingit settled in "a bay above Cape Spencer where much glacial ice collected," today's Glacier Bay.[xxxiii]

The younger sister is said to have headed South and become mother of the Haida. At Louise Island, on the leeward side of Haida Gwai'i, this Louise may still walk ancient towns like **Kona**. Europeans called this town Skedans after a Haida name for the chief meaning "from his daughter". Neighbouring clans with the Hawaiian-sounding names of Djiguashi-lana'i and Kahai'i-lana'i all claimed to be descended from one woman. (On the island of Hawaii, Kona also means leeward.) The Haida clan of Kona-kegawai'i settled here and turned Kona into a centre of seaborne trade.

Though the wooden clan houses of **Kona** are now in ruins, we can still see their foundations. The totem poles still remain as ghostly guardians. We are reminded that smallpox and measles took more than 90% of the people here. With their lives went genetic evidence of where the Haida originated and where they voyaged. Walking through these towns, we find signs of their presence.

Archeologists have found stone fishtraps and clam gardens in the waters near Haida Gwai'i. Many of these structures, built from thousands of stones, were hidden until recently by rising seas. The Northwest First Nations raised and harvested seafood and clams. In addition to hunting and gathering, they practiced an early form of aquaculture.

More than 1000 fish traps have been found in the Northwest, in places like Desolation Sound and the Sliammon Reserve. The Glenrose Cannery site near Vancouver contains a fish trap from 2600 BC.[xxxiv] Also at Glenrose the earliest known human figure from the Northwest was found.

With his topknot hairdo and Asian features, this man appears to have arrived from across the Pacific.

Wrangell

Petroglyphs, pictures carved in stone, were created by more than one prehistoric culture. **Petroglyph Beach** near Wrangell, Alaska, has the biggest collection of them in the world. More petroglyphs can be seen on the coast of Vancouver Island. Carving pictures in solid rock required considerable effort. Most of these petroglyphs face toward the sea--their origins, purpose and even age still mysteries.

From the time around 4000 BC the modern culture of the Northwest developed. The shell middens grew larger, and large-scale fishing of salmon began. The cedar tree first took root here about the same time. As the climate warmed, great forests grew. Near Icy Strait and Glacier Bay archeologists have found remains of a wooden house 3750 years old.[xxxv] Archeologists call this the Developmental Stage, when the Northwest peoples flowered.

The Northwest clan house is a classic design. It is built from wooden planks shaped with an *adze*. Four carved posts mark the corners. The front wall is painted with the colourful designs of the clan. Another carved post marks the entrance, which always faces the water. Inside, a decorative wooden screen dominates the room. Multiple generations lived together in these clan houses. John Muir visited the Chief Shakes House in Wrangell and was made an honourary chief. The Whale House of the Chilkat is world-famous for its carvings. The Alishan tribal house built in faraway Taiwan may have been influenced from Alaska. The design of the clan house would spread across the Pacific.

Ketchikan

Ketchikan is a destination for eagles and bears, "Salmon Capitol of the World". A salmon stream runs through the town, past the bawdy houses of Creek Street. The Tlinkit village of Saxman is just 2 miles south of Ketchikan. The beautiful clan house faces the water amid a park full of totem poles. Visitors to Ketchikan should not miss a chance to visit Saxman and be welcomed to a *potlatch* ceremony. The potlatches are occasions for different tribes to get together. **Totem Bight State Park** in Ketchikan contains another clan house with totem poles.

The Alaska Haida are descended from ancestors who lived on Langara Island, the northernmost land of Haida Gwai'i. In their oral history, some fishermen on a beach discovered a finely carved pole which had drifted from across the sea. In another version of the story, a woman picking berries found the pole near Rose Spit. From this example, the Haida carved two poles just like it, the Northwest's first totem poles. This story has a ring of truth, for Europeans saw totem poles on Langara Island before they were seen elsewhere.[xxxvi] About a century before Europeans arrived, these Haida crossed Dixon Entrance to live in Alaska.

European missionaries thought that totem poles were idols to be burned. Over time, many totem poles have been lost or left to rot. At the Totem Heritage Center in Ketchikan, abandoned poles are gathered and restored. In a culture without a formal written language, totem poles are a record of history and ancestors.

Nature's totem pole, the double helix of DNA also carries a record of our ancestors. Told together, these stories show how mitochondrial DNA spreads by the female line. A seafaring man arrived in Ka-Houpo-o-Kane before a great flood. Taking his wife, he escaped in a canoe carved from a log. A man and a woman arrived in Haida Gwai'i, where the man was killed but the woman survived. A woman had two daughters, who each married men from the interior. The daughters became clan mothers of Tlingit and Haida, who in turn founded clans and moieties within those tribes. A totem pole drifted from across the sea, and from its example two copies were made which started a tradition. The clan of Ina, with DNA sequences numbered 189 217 and 189 217 261, spread from the Taiwan region to America.

The Haida became famous for their finely carved canoes. They had experience and endless red cedar forests to build from. The canoes were often carved with elaborate figures. European explorers found the Haida using iron tools, which anthropologists think came from Asia in prehistoric times.[xxxvii] Thor Heyerdahl suggested that two canoes might have been lashed together to create a catamaran, but that is not needed. Haida canoes are very stable and difficult to capsize. The canoes could cut through small waves and float over the big ones. Today this 63-foot Haida canoe has traveled to New York's American Museum of Natural History.

One day a Haida war party in two canoes ventured north from Prince George Island to raid Tlingit villages, but found no booty. Finally they decided to meet with the Tlingit to trade, then one of the Haida fell in love with the daughter of a Tlingit chief. In exchange for permission to marry her, the Haida gave the chief one of their fine canoes. Forever after Tlingit traded with Haida for the canoes.[xxxviii] Two-piece fishhooks, similar to Polynesian fishhooks, have been found in both Haida Gwai'i and Vancouver Island. Fishhooks are considered proof of seaborne travel across Queen Charlotte Sound.[xxxix]

Though their clan mothers travelled separate ways, Tlingit and Haida still have much in common. They share the matrilineal clan system--identity comes from the mother's clan. In modern meetings the Haida have given the Tlingit first place, in deference to the older sister from Dall Island. During 1935 the Central Council of the Tlingit and Haida Indian Tribes of Alaska was formed to represent their interests. Today, Tlingit and Haida are legally one. Their joint website, ccthita.org, proudly mentions their voyages to Hawaii.

Vancouver Island

Between Haida Gwai'i and Vancouver Island is the great opening of Queen Charlotte Sound. Stories of the Raven have flown here too. In a local legend Kane-a-keluh was a wandering hero who transformed into a Raven to bring men fire. He is said to have married a woman from across the ocean, then sailed away never to be seen again. Thor Heyerdahl thought that Kane-a-keluh was the genesis of the Polynesian Kane, an idea whose truth may be hidden in the fog.

We can't be certain from which port the first voyage to Hawaii sailed from. Heyerdahl speculated that it began in a valley near the Hakai'i channel, possibly stopping at the north tip of Vancouver Island. The oral history left by Solomon Peleioholani tells of the first Hawaiians coming from Alaska.

I have found a likely port of Chief Nuu. Since camping there as a child I've enjoyed the beauty of Vancouver Island. The windswept Pacific coast is home to the Nuu-chah-nulth. When Captain Cook encountered them in 1778, he wrote their name as Nootka and called their home waters Nootka Sound. The first encounter between Europeans and the Northwest's First Nations went so well that Cook named the place Friendly Cove. The settlement called Yuquot or "wind that blows in all directions" has been inhabited over 4,000 years, longer than Rome. DNA testing has found the Polynesian clan of Ina widespread among the Nuu-chah-nulth.

The Nuu-chah-nulth presented Cook with a finely carved wooden club, which is in a museum at University of British Columbia. It is so similar to a Polynesian club that another museum labeled it as Hawaiian. Though the northwest peoples knew of the bow and arrow, they never used them in war. Cook's artist George Weber was able to sketch both the exterior and interiors of native houses.

Of all the peoples of British Columbia, the Nuu-chah-nulth were most accustomed to the open sea and the only mariners who pursued the great whales. The Omega-3 and fatty acids of whale meat were a nutritious feast. Nuu-chah-nulth believed in a close bond with the whales. Long training in the wilderness, fasting, spiritual preparation and elaborate rituals prepared crews for sailing. The crew's status in society was similar to today's astronauts. Chiefs were sea captains who gained status from how many whales they could bring from the sea. The whale strengthened relationships with other tribes, for people would sail great distances to form alliances and marriages. When Nuu-chah-nulth were lost at sea, they would pray to the whales for guidance.

Mysterious whaling rituals were staged in the **Yuquot Whaler's Shrine**. This wooden structure contains 88 full-sized carved human figures, 4 carved whales and 16 real human skulls! During 1903, while most of the Nuu-chah-nulth were away at sea, someone paid 500 dollars and spirited the Shrine away. It is presently in the dark basement of an American museum. In 2016 the premier of British Columbia petitioned to bring the Shrine back into the light. It could be an attraction comparable to the Warriors of Xi'an.

Nuu-chah-nulth canoes were designed for long voyages. Like Captain Cook's ships, the canoes had flat bottoms which made them easy to land and load with cargo. A high bow and vertical stern allowed the canoe to be beached stern-first, with the protected bow facing the waves. The wide stern also provided a comfortable seat for a steersman or woman on long trips. The gunwales (sides) were angled out about 30 degrees, making the canoes extremely stable. The typical length of 35-40 feet is ideal for the open ocean. A Nuu-chah-nulth canoe could travel over and between the waves without being swamped or broken.

The canoes routinely ventured over 40 miles offshore, spending many nights in the open sea. Women regularly travelled across the straits between Yuquot and Puget Sound when the men were away. Nuu-chah-nulth canoes could travel at 6-7 knots, while Captain Cook's ships struggled to exceed 5 knots. With favourable currents a canoe could cover about 150 miles per day.[xl] A typical oceangoing canoe carried a crew of eight—just right for Nuu, his wife, their three adult sons and three wives.

Nuu-chah-nulth women kept the best record of Pacific voyages, for they preserved learning in songs. These songs contained their knowledge of the Kuroshio Current, which they called Klin Otto or Dark Tide. According to oral history Nuu-chah-nulth ancestors arrived in the Northwest 15,000 years ago, close to modern estimates for America's first people. Even navigational directions were in songs, sung by the steerswomen while at sea. These women could navigate canoes by the stars or by currents if the stars were hidden. Nuu-chah-nulth knew a song for reaching the Big Island--they may have been first to call Hawaii the Big Island. Much of this oral history, including voyages to Hawaii, was nearly lost. These songs were entrusted to and preserved by women[xli].

Discovery: 230 BC

Aided by eagles, I entered the Whale House of the Chilkat. Its carvings are in a heritage centre that opened in 2016. There I saw wood sculptures nearly as old as Michelangelo. The windows look out over a river filled with eagles. About 2,000 years ago a Tlingit man from Prince of Wales Island, along with his four nephews, followed the eagles north to their mysterious Winter destination.

Across the mountains from Glacier Bay they discovered the Chilkat River Valley, where to this day thousands of eagles gather each November. Due to an underwater source of warmth, the river does not freeze, and teems with spawning salmon late in the year. Eagles and the humans following them enjoy a November feast. The valley is also one of the few land routes into North America, a location as strategic as Hawaii is for the Pacific. The man and his nephews founded Klukwan, one of the most important Tlingit settlements. Discovery of the Chilkat River Valley was a canoe trip of many days, like a voyage to Hawaii.

Given the wonders we have seen, no one can ignore that seagoing people thrived in Alaska and the Northwest by 4000 BC and probably far earlier. Their ancestors voyaged thousands of miles from the region near Taiwan. America's first people carved complex societies, admirable works of art, and seagoing canoes. They regularly travelled the sea as far as the Aleutian Islands and California. Some seagoing peoples developed a relationship with the migrating whales. The record of their voyages was maintained in song. Very likely they followed currents and whales deeper into the Pacific. They needed only the inspiration and the will.

***Inspiration*:** Like the biblical story of the Flood, the oral history of Mr. Alaska and Woman of Dreams was passed on for thousands of years. The island continent Ka-Houpo-o-Kane was part of that history. Navigation lessons would have included the latitude of Ka-Houpo-o-Kane, which could be found by the angle of stars from the horizon. As they huddled indoors during Alaskan Winters, Tlingit and Haida remembered tales of a warmer land across the sea. Among the Tlingit I have worked and spoken with, they are unanimous in the tradition that ancient Alaskans discovered Hawaii, traveling there many times.

***Will*:** The story of Hawaii's discovery is stuff of future novels. Nuu might have been born Tlingit or Haida, the son of seagoing people. In Hawaiian genealogy he was son to Lalo of Kona, making him a descendant of the two sisters on Dall Island, Alaska. The town of Kona in Haida Gwai'i was a gathering place of seagoing canoes. Like the later Columbus, Nuu crossed an inland sea to find his ship. Mastering the arduous training of the Nuu-chah-nulth would make Nuu Chief and Captain. Finding his own woman of dreams, Lili-noe, in Vancouver Island preserved the clan of Ina and its DNA. If genetics favour a Canadian port, Nuu and his family may have voyaged in a whaling canoe.

This was **Ka-waa-halau-alii-o-ka-moku**, grandly named "Royal Canoe of the Continent" and first ship to reach Hawaii. She was about 40 feet long, carved from a single log. She had a crew of exactly eight, men and women. Her great voyage, one of the most important in history, brought the first humans to the Hawaiian Islands and started an age of exploration. It took place around the year 230 BC.

At sea Nuu led from the bow, vigilant for signs of land. Lili-noe steered with an oar like many Nuu-chah-nulth women had done before her. Their three sons and three wives rowed, singing to keep rhythm and morale. At night the tired rowers slept, perchance to dream of faraway lands. Nuu and Lili-noe, restless, watched the distant stars while currents silently carried them forward. The tracks of whales led voyagers west.

Our journey around Alaska and the Northwest shows that oral history has a basis in fact. In Glacier Bay we can see change, the return of life, and a Kelp Highway from Asia. Pacific currents would have brought voyagers ashore on Haida Gwai'i, where a Raven could have found them on the beach at Rose Spit. In a cave on Dall Island, clan mothers of Tlingit and Haida might have lived. Seagoing tribes settled in towns from Kona in Haida Gwai'i to Klukwan in the Chilkat River Valley and across the West. Among the Haida, Tlingit and Nuu-chah-nulth we have seen the canoes that ventured into currents would have brought voyagers ashore on Haida Gwai'i, where a Raven may have found them at Rose Spit. In a cave on Dall Island, clan mothers of Tlingit and Haida might have lived. Seagoing tribes settled in towns from Kona in Haida Gwai'i to Klukwan in the Chilkat River Valley and across the West. Among the Haida, Tlingit and Nuu-chah-nulth we have seen the canoes that ventured into the Pacific. Currents and winds take us to the homeland.

The Alaskan State flag features the Big Dipper and Polaris, the North Star. The Big Dipper also forms the tail and hindquarters of Ursa Major, the Great Bear. In ancient times Ursa Major was symbol of a tribe living on Auke Bay, near today's capitol Juneau. When another Tlingit tribe took over this land, they adopted the symbol and display it on their crests to this day.

The flag design was created by a native Alaskan Aleut, a seventh grader named Benny Benson. When Benny was three years old his mother died of pneumonia and Benny was sent to an orphanage. One night, while dreaming of his father away at sea, he remembered his mother telling him about the stars. The father, an experienced fisherman like many Aleut, could find his way home using the North Star. The next day Benny Benson designed the flag we see today.

As depicted in the flag, the forward two stars of the Big Dipper point to Polaris. The North Star also marks the tail of Ursa Minor, the Little Bear. In Hawaii the Big Dipper is called Na Hiku and Polaris is *Hokopa'a*, the fixed star because the other stars appear to revolve around it. The angle of the North Star from the horizon equals the observer's latitude from the equator.

HAWAII

HOMELAND

June 17, 2017

They were at sea without a compass, but were not lost. They steered by the stars and waves, aided by visits from helpful birds. In three years at sea they knew the way. The week before they had sighted Mount Haleakala on Maui, their first glimpse of the Hawaiian Islands. Soon the island of Maui was to port and the Big Island to starboard as the canoe sailed through Alenuihaha Channel. Turning northwest, the canoe rounded Maui until Oahu and Diamond Head were in sight. A white city of skyscrapers grew above Waikiki Beach. Hundreds of boats sailed out to greet the canoe. At Magic Island more than 50,000 people were gathered. After orbiting the Earth, *Hokulea* had returned home.

Hokulea is named for the star also called Arcturus, which passes over the latitude of Hawaii. The voyaging canoe, based upon traditional designs, was built with modern materials. *Hokulea's* voyages have tested the traditions of our ancestors voyaging the Pacific. During 1976 and again in 1980 she sailed to Tahiti and back without modern navigational aids. This year of 2017 she completed a round-the-world voyage lasting three years, about as long as one of Captain Cook's voyages. *Hokulea* has also created a new sense of pride among island peoples, for we were voyagers.

The Big Island

I am writing this from a home on the Big Island. Hawaii has not always been my home, but since coming here as a child it has felt like home. Today about 200,000 people call the Big Island home, though there were once many more. High Chief Solomon Peleioholani grew up extremely close to here—I heard the stories he left us. Our Hawaiian Islands have much to explore, of which I can only describe a sample.

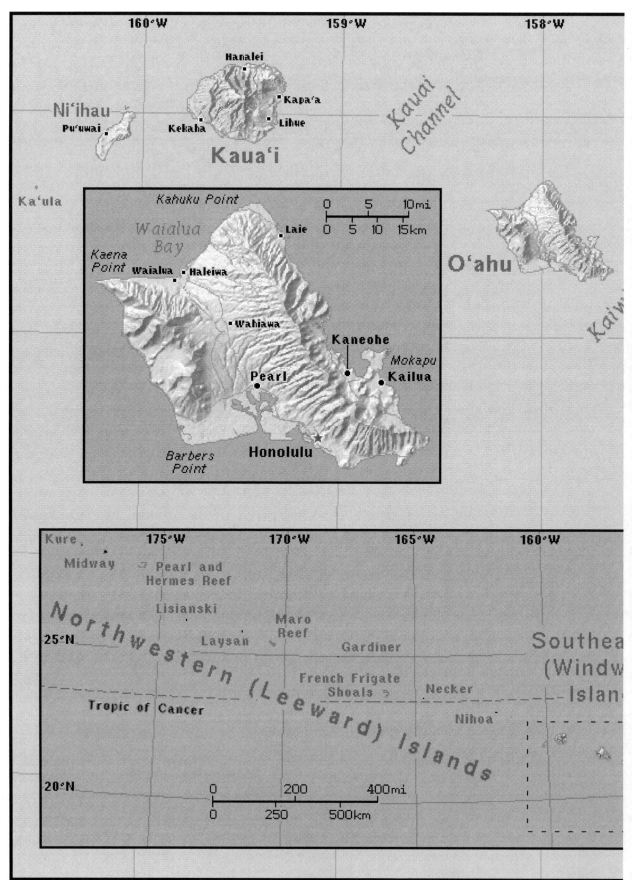

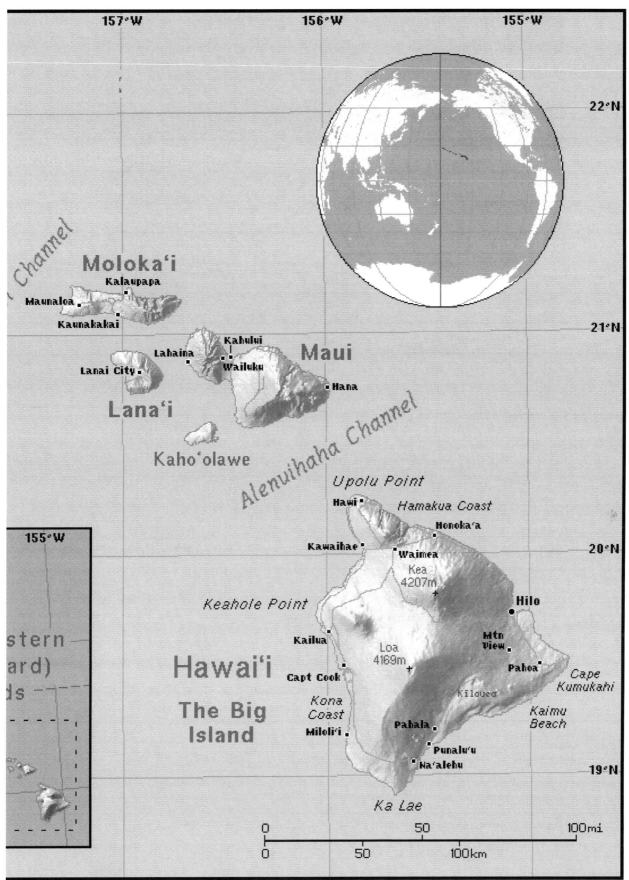

Hawaii is the youngest land in the world and still in a process of creation. Our Islands formed over a plume of lava originating deep within the Earth. Geologists think it originates at the boundary between Earth's core and mantle. The Pacific Plate has been slowly sliding northwest over this hotspot, causing the Islands to form one by one. Kauai, oldest of the major islands, is about 4-5 million years old. The Big Island is the youngest, barely one million years and still growing.

The Big Island grows atop several immense volcanoes, with smaller volcanic craters in between. The tallest is dormant Mauna Kea at 14,060 feet. From the sea floor the White Mountain measures 30,000 feet, taller than Everest. Mauna Loa and Kilauea have recently been active. Lava flows every day from Kilauea, the most active volcano on Earth.

To the southeast a new island called Lo'ihi is erupting beneath the sea, and will emerge in mere thousands of years.

Northeasterly tradewinds bring moisture which piles into the island to end as snow atop Mauna Kea. The air atop the summit is clean of turbulence and pollutants, making it an ideal place for astronomers' observatories. The White Mountain can be seen from many miles away. Snow-capped Mauna Kea would have been the first land sighted by Nuu from the prow of his canoe.

Rainbow Falls just outside Hilo are a spectacular sight. Hilo is one of the rainiest towns in the US with 140 inches per year. The Big Island's windward side is lush with gardens and waterfalls. The Falls reputedly conceal a cave where the demigod Maui lived along with his mother, the goddess Hina.

Many days I have enjoyed hiking **Volcanoes National Park**. I was allowed to walk the floor of the immense Kilauea Caldera and peer into Halemaumau Crater in its floor. Every night the crater glows red. On the caldera's rim Steaming Cliffs leak vapor every day. A short walk away Sulfur Springs give off a smell like rotten eggs. I've walked to Pu'u O'o vent, source of the current eruption.

Chain of Craters Road winds through miles of lava fields toward the sea before the road is blocked by more lava. Hiking from the end of the road, I've seen lava from Pu'u O'o dumping into the Pacific. Here the lava solidifies and creates new land. Over time living things will take hold and add to our Island. I've walked through tubes created by lava flows that melt through rock to create caves. The Big Island's hidden passages are an adventure to explore.

Partway down Chain of Craters Road are the **Pu'u Loa** petroglyphs. They are extremely similar to the petroglyphs we saw facing the ocean from Alaska. Walking through both places gives the impression that distant peoples were trying to communicate.

Hawaiian traditions say that the art of carving petroglyphs came from across the sea. Petroglyphs have been carved in Southeast Alaska, Hawaii, the Marquesas Islands and New Zealand. They have not been found in the western Pacific atolls of Melanesia and Micronesia, where the first Polynesians were once thought to have passed. They are not found west of the Polynesian Triangle, or west of a line drawn from Hawaii to New Zealand. Rock carvings have been found in Southeast Asia, but not in the scattered islands in between. We can read one message from the petroglyphs of Alaska and Hawaii: the artists did not arrive from the West.

Polynesian voyagers are proud of following winds and currents, all of which lead here from North America. Trade winds blow here from Alaska. The circulating North Pacific Gyre turns southward from Alaska to become the California Current, which then veers west. These rivers of air and water lead to the island of Hawaii.

Upon sighting Hawaii, voyagers would need a place to land. As Captain Cook would find, most of the windward coast is too rugged for an anchorage. If Nuu and Lili-noe steered toward Mauna Kea, they would have found Waipio Valley and the welcoming beach of this book's cover. Spectacular waterfalls, like the 1200-foot Hi'ilawe Falls, tumble from precipitous cliffs to join the Waipio River. Of all green places on the windward side, this was the greenest. To voyagers from Alaska, Waipio Valley was the Garden of Eden.

Chief Nuu, like the later Columbus, may have set out to reach Asia. Lessons of navigators would have taught Nuu to find the latitude of Taiwan or lost Ka-Houpo-o-Kane. Since the Hawaiian Islands are at the same latitude, navigation stars would have brought Nuu and Lili-noe here. The paradise of Hawaii and Waipio Valley would have been their reward.

The women of Vancouver Island remember this journey. Nuu-chah-nulth set out to find the land of their ancestors, a place of the rising Sun, which they thought was a paradise. At sea, they replenished their food supply with floating kelp, which is abundant on America's west coast. When there was no wind, every available man and woman took up oars and rowed. After a voyage of many days, they landed at a place that looked like paradise. They washed in streams of fresh water, which only flows from the Big Island's windward side. They found trees full of fresh fruit, like the native *pandanus* trees of Waipio Valley. Slowly they realised that they were the only people on the island; it was not the same paradise they set out to find. Some of these voyagers remained on the island but others ventured farther into the Pacific. The first voyage to Hawaii is remembered on both sides of the ocean[xlii].

Since a time long forgotten, Waipio Valley has been home to Hawaii's chiefs and kings. In times of famine, the lush Valley could always provide crops. Today tasty pink guava fruits grow here like weeds. Kamehameha the Great and Solomon Peleioholani spent part of their childhoods near Waipio Valley. The graves of many Hawaiian chiefs are hidden in the surrounding hills. We cannot disturb their resting places, but we can follow their history.

Hawaiian genealogies record Lili-noe as an important ancestor, buried in a cave on the slopes of Mauna Kea. She is said to live on as a goddess of the mist. We see Lili-noe's misty fingers nearly every *Kohola* are the humpback whales and Kohola-lele means leaping humpback whale. In finding Hawaii, voyagers found where the whales migrate each Winter. The whales release a mucus-like substance known as *hupe kohola*. Tiny fish breed within this stuff. On beaches near the cliffs of Kohola-lele, Hawaiians gathered these clear sacs for the fish that breed within them. Hawaii is a place where *Kohola* may be born safe from Orca predators, for the "killer whale" only rarely travels here.

These waters are the playground of Orca's cousins in the dolphin family. **Spinner dolphins** frequently swim with us in the waters of Kealakekua Bay, or accompany our dive boats off the Kona coast. Many times I have encountered dolphins while diving. Spotted dolphins and bottlenose dolphins are seen farther from the shore. The dolphins' intelligence is legend—like the Orcas, dolphins cooperate to herd fish.

We've encountered another brainy creature near the Big Island, the **Manta Ray**. Of all fish, Mantas have the largest brains for their size. We know very little about the life of Mantas--we don't know where they spawn or if they migrate. I have met many of them at night off the Kona Coast, where they are equally curious about us. One of the best spots for an encounter is Keauhou Bay.

At sunset, our group descended in scuba gear carrying diving lights. Our divemaster, an experienced diver, had to turn back due to difficulty pressurizing. Finally reaching the bottom, we sat in a circle and pointed our lights upward. The lights draw plankton which attracts Mantas. This is a trade— Mantas get a meal and we get a look. Sitting around a light in the darkness is our oldest form of meeting.

First one Manta glided into view, then another. Soon they filled our circle of light, effortlessly banking and looping through the water. With a wingspan that approaches 23 feet, Mantas are a majestic sight. The curious Mantas swam straight for my face, so close that I could see into their huge mouths and down their throats, before deftly climbing away and missing me by an inch. There is nothing to fear, for Mantas have no stinger and eat only tiny sea creatures. This ritual has been practised over the years by both sides, true Close Encounters of the Third Kind. Someday we may encounter life like this on a distant water world. Their form of intelligence may be inscrutable, but we can work out ways of meeting.

To its discoverers Hawaii was a new world, formed less than one million years. They saw no bears or wolves, for Hawaii has no indigenous land mammals. The native *pandanus* tree provided them with fruits to eat and bark to make cloth. They found berries to gather, called *ohelo* and *akala*. Lacking the salmon streams of Alaska, settlers would need other ways to gather fish. Even the black sand beach of Waipio Valley seemed unearthly.

On hikes I've seen the **Nene** or Hawaiian Goose, the State bird. They are descended from Canadian Geese that arrived around 500,000 years ago. Until recently the Nene has been endangered, but they are slowly returning to the wild.

The culture of these first Hawaiians has been a mystery. They appear to have worshipped no formal gods, but believed in family and harmony with nature. Their clans were identified with animals like the Shark Clan or Eel Clan. The beliefs of the earliest Hawaiian clans were similar to those of Native Alaskans.[xliii]

Legendary Chief Nuu would not be the last voyager to find Hawaii. A family of eight would not be large or diverse enough to found a colony. At some point Nuu or his descendants must have voyaged back, to tell everyone what they had found and gather more settlers. From similarities in society, culture, art, woodcarving and tools, we have seen many hints of connection. To return canoes could travel north to pass the North Pacific High, a wind blowing from the California coast. They could then turn east to run before this wind that blows at 40 degrees north latitude in Summer and 25 degrees north in Winter. The westerly wind could carry them back to America. Like the canoes that ventured thousands of miles down the American coast, others travelled between newfound Hawaii and the mainland.

    Hawaiian history tells of Lua Nuu, a descendant of ten generations after Chief Nuu. He is said to have sought a high place to perform a sacrifice for his god, but none of the Hawaiian mountains was tall enough. According to this story Lua Nuu voyaged eastward and found "a sharp-peaked hill projecting precipitously into the ocean," a fine description of Mount Fairweather near Glacier Bay. Reaching higher above the sea than Mauna Kea, this mountain was exactly what Lua Nuu was looking for. He is said to have stayed and named the land Aina Lau'ana-a-Kane or Great Land of Kane. The similar name Alaska also means "Great Land". Lua Nuu is said to have married a woman from the "Nawao" tribe and become father of the Menehune, a people from whom early Hawaiians are descended from.

Seven generations later Lua Nuu's descendant Hawai'iloa lived in the Great Land of Kane. The land farther to the North was then known as "Great Ulu".[xliv] He was the Hawai'iloa said to have fished the seas and discovered our Islands. He had a brother named Ki who settled Tahiti and another brother named Kana Loa who discovered the Marquesas Islands. With an average generation of 21 years, Hawai'iloa would have voyaged around 50 AD. Chief Nuu, Hawai'iloa, and Captain Cook may all have found Hawaii, only in different centuries. Other voyagers throughout time, hopefully including readers of this book, have discovered our Islands.

Seven generations after Hawai'iloa, Princess Papa-hanaumoku, also called Haumea, married High Chief Wakea. Their followers called Wakea the Sky Father and Princess Papa the Earth Mother. In fact they were human rulers who began a new genealogy. Marrying Princess Papa, a descendant of the first Hawaiians, cemented Wakea's claim to the throne and spread DNA from the clan of Ina. One researcher has connected the time of Wakea with a comet which appeared in 178 AD, and with a supernova seen near Alpha and Beta Centauri in 185 AD.[xlv] This astronomy would fit with genealogy, which places High Chief Wakea 24 generations or about 500 years after Chief Nuu.

Waipio Valley would not be the only place voyagers would land. Like Rose Spit on Haida Gwai'i, the beach is wracked by dangerous winds and rip tides. Settlers on the Big Island would need a safe place to tie their canoes, sheltered from the winds. Sailing South we can reach the leeward, or Kona side.

Kamilo Beach is named for the swirling currents that come ashore here. Like Rose Spit, this beach accumulates lots of debris. Today plastic bottles litter the shore, and volunteers are needed to clean them up. Ancient canoe builders watched this shore for logs drifting from the North. Douglas fir, red cedar, and redwood were known to be superior to Hawaiian logs. We can be certain that canoes from North America voyaged to Hawaii, because they arrived while still logs.

Another traveler ended up on our supper table. The **sweet potato** first grew in Central and South America. Sweet potatoes don't sprout in the tropics on their own, and must be cultivated. Sweet potato samples found in Tahiti were dated to 1000 AD, long before Europeans arrived.[xlvi] *Kumara* is the word for sweet potato in today's New Zealand and also in the Quechua language of the Andes. Presence of the *kumara* is considered proof of voyaging from America to Pacific islands.

Ka Lae or "South Point" is the Southernmost land in 50 United States. The Pacific trade winds blow past the Big Island here, making it a very breezy place! This is not Hawaii's first settlement, for it is not a good place to farm. The winds blow so hard and constant that trees grow sideways. South Point has grown wind farms, where giant white turbines spin for clean energy. At times Ka Lae has been proposed as a spaceport, because rockets launched closer to the equator get an extra boost from Earth's spin. West of Ka Lae, sheltered from the winds, we can see holes drilled in the rocks by ancient voyagers to anchor canoes.

A very rugged road leads to the **Papa-kolea Green Sand Beach**, a unique place for a swim. The green sand is a product of the volcanoes, a mineral called olivine. I became intimately familiar with olivine due to my work at NASA, for it appears in Moon samples I examined from Apollo missions. Something else from far away lands nearby.

Papa-kolea Beach is named for the **Kolea**—the same Pacific Golden Plovers we saw nesting in Alaska! During Winter the *Kolea* rest in parks and lawns all over Hawaii and the South Pacific. These little birds, even newly-born infants, somehow navigate all the way from Alaska each year. The Kolea feathers are not waterproof, so they must fly the Pacific nonstop. Their fossils tell us that the Kolea have been following this itinerary for 120,000 years. Islanders have long known that they breed across the sea--an old chant translates to, "The egg of the Kolea is laid in a foreign land." Voyagers following these birds would be led to Hawaii.

The Big Island was once nest of the *Alala*, or Hawaiian crow. Like their Raven cousins *Alala* are quite smart, even fashioning tools to catch food. They were the closest Hawaiian relatives to Ravens of the North, but hunting and habitat loss caused the last wild *Alala* to die in 2002. During 2016 a family raised in captivity was released in the Big Island, in hope that the *Alala* will return.

The first Hawaiians had never seen chickens, cattle or *Pua'a* the pig. The Big Island would not be a pig island for centuries. Early settlers from Alaska did bring one good friend:

The Hawaiian **Poi dog** has the upright ears typical of Alaskan Spitz breeds. Its legs are short, its teeth are unused to meat, and it rarely barks. The poi dog is the result of generations of dogs being fed a diet of poi, the grey paste made from taro. In a land without pigs, chickens or cows, getting meat from a dog was easier than feeding meat into a dog. The poi dogs did not die out, but interbreeding with other dogs caused the breed to disappear. The Poi dog's DNA is hidden in today's dogs.

Near the tip of South Point is the *heiau* of **Kalalea**. Hawaiian *heiau* are rock temples built for various purposes, from honouring gods to navigation. The outer walls of this *heiau* are aligned with the four points of the compass. Navigational stones here point to Tahiti and Rapa Nui (Easter Island). Hawaiian navigators leaving for these islands sighted these stones to set a course. According to the family who were caretakers here, the *heiau* has been visited by the Polynesian Voyaging Society and by Maori of today's New Zealand, all seeking the paths of their ancestors.[xlvii]

Navigators were always able to point toward the place they started from. They would get their heading from the navigational stones until the stones disappeared below the horizon, then rely on the stars.

Navigators developed a star compass with at least sixteen points, tied to rising and setting stars. They would trail a rope full of knots to estimate their speed. Using a mental system of dead reckoning, navigators could always determine where they were. One secret of navigation is knowing the way home.

West of South Point is the ancient village of Pu'u Ali'i. In 1953 a young woman from a nearby village found some strange fishhooks buried in a sand dune, which she brought to the archeologists of the Bishop Museum. Some of the fishhooks from Pu'u Ali'i were dated as early as 124 AD.[xlviii] A sample of used charcoal from a fire here was tentatively dated to 300 BC, the time of Chief Nuu.[xlix] Pu'u Ali'i is one of the oldest human sites in Hawaii.

Moana fans will remember Maui's fishhook found hidden in a cave. Archeologists have found hundreds of fishhooks in Pu'u Ali'i. Two-piece fishhooks appeared in Hawaii but not in other Polynesian islands. They were once thought to be a Hawaiian invention, but already existed in North America. In 1947 New York's American Museum of Natural History displayed Northwest and Polynesian fishhooks together, showing them nearly identical.

Another ancient settlement, Waiahukini is the last safe anchorage before rounding South Point. In 1954 a lava tube shelter was discovered here.[l] This shelter is filled with shell middens, like Kit'n'Kaboodle Cave in Dall Island. The remains of a sea urchin found here were dated as early as 60 BC.[li] The lava tube at Waiahukini contains over a thousand fishhooks.

Many archeological sites on the Big Island date from before 300 AD.[lii] A piece of charcoal found while building a hotel near Waikoloa was dated to about the same time.[liii] Another cave in Keauhou has been dated to about 54 AD, the time Hawai'iloa is said to have arrived in the Islands.[liv] An archeology textbook "with firm evidence" places the first people on Hawaii before 300 AD, the time of High Chief Wakea.[lv] An authority on petroglyphs concludes that they arrived with Hawaii's first settlers before 300 AD.[lvi] Herb Kane, artist/designer of *Hokulea* and one of the founders of the Polynesian Voyaging Society, estimated that settlement happened before 100 AD.[lvii] These early dates caused a rethinking of Polynesian history.[lviii]

Kealakekua Bay, where spinner dolphins play, has some of the best snorkeling reefs on the island. This Bay was created when a section of the island broke off and fell into the sea. The resulting tsunami completely inundated the island of Kahoolawe, 1483 feet high. On the shore of Kealakekua Bay is a single white obelisk. It is the monument to Captain Cook, whose voyages ended here.

The Hapaiali'i Heiau near Keauhou was solar calendar. Like Stonehenge, the stones here could be used to predict Summer and Winter solstices. The Keauhou area also contains a bobsled track! Somehow Hawaii's first people had learned to race sleds called *holua*. Building a sled track was a big project, and this sport was reserved for chiefs.

Kailua-Kona is the site of King Kamehameha's *heiau*. Kamehameha the Great is a revolutionary figure, the first to unite all the islands under his rule. As a young man Kamehameha visited Captain Cook's ships. He was famed for his physical strength, bravery and wisdom. Because Kamehameha was from the Big Island, our archipelago is now known as the Hawaiian Islands or just Hawaii. This peaceful *heiau* was Kamehameha's home in the sunset of his life. Kona means leeward, as it does in Haida Gwai'i.

The Kaloko Fishpond is just north of Kona. It was built from thousands of stones, like the fish traps of the Pacific Northwest. Hawaii presents a similar challenge to archeologists as the coast of Alaska, for the seaside homes of the earliest settlers are covered by rising seas. Fishponds have been found in Alaska and Hawaii, but not in the islands farther South. More than just traps, these ponds raised and bred fish. Along with the Haida, early Hawaiians practiced a form of aquaculture.

The first Hawaiians did not, of course, call themselves "Hawaiians". They were called *Kanaka Maori*, or first people. Our tour around the Big Island has revealed their signs. In Waipio Valley and South Point we can see where ancient mariners landed. They left us petroglyphs, fish traps, temples and navigational stones pointing farther south.

Whales were important to these first Hawaiians. King Kamehameha was told that he would rule all the Islands if he built a temple atop **Pu'u Kohola**, Hill of the Whales. The hill was already the site of the Malekini Heiau, an ancient temple built by Hawaii's earliest inhabitants. Another nearby *heiau*, said to be devoted to sharks, is today underwater. Kamehameha was not known for building on top of other people's temples, so he built his *heiau* farther up the hill. From this hill we can see whales arrive from Alaska.

Farther North is the **Maka-o-hule** Navigation Heiau. Like Kalalea, this *heiau* was used to train navigators. Standing stones here point to Tahiti and the Marquesas Islands. While exploring this *heiau* I found two smaller stones on a separate level. They point directly to Point Arena in California, nearest point on America's west coast. Anyone seeing this place will have no doubt that Hawaiians knew the way to these other lands, for no such navigational stones have been found in Tahiti or the Marquesas.

Near the North tip of the Big Island, close to Kamehameha's birthplace, is the enormous **Mo'okini heiau**. The main structure is 250 feet long and 125 feet wide, with walls 30 feet thick. Descendants of the priest Kuamo'o Mo'okini, who arrived from across the ocean, still watch over this *heiau*. According to Hawaiian and Mo'okini family tradition the *heiau* was started in 480 AD. Some stories say that Kuamo'o Mo'okini came from as far as the Middle East. For people to have built such a structure in 480 AD, Hawaii must have been settled long before then.

Mo'okini heiau was enlarged and re-dedicated around 1200 AD by another priest named Pa'ao. His arrival from the Tahitian Islands, after an argument with his older brother that led to murder, started a dark chapter of history. Pa'ao thought that Hawaiian culture was too decadent for his tastes. He was shocked to see Hawaii's chiefs marrying commoners. Pa'ao sailed to the island of Raiatea to find a chief he approved of. Raiatea was then centre of a strict religion, with ambitious chiefs eager to spread it by force. Pa'ao returned to Hawaii with a Samoan Chief named Pili, and canoes full of warriors. The imposing Pili became King of the Island of Hawaii.

The new *Ali'i* or chiefs introduced the strict *kapu* system, which made many things off-limits. Men could no longer dine with women. Commoners could no longer look at chiefs--even standing in a chief's shadow was punishable by death. To maintain the purity of their bloodlines, these new chiefs freely married brothers to sisters. If the moieties of Raven and Eagle were remembered, they would have been erased along with the culture of the first Hawaiians. The story of Hawaii's first discovery became a secret known to just a few high chiefs. Anyone doubting the words of a High Chief like Solomon Peleioholani would have a very short life.

Both Europeans and Polynesians have at times been guilty of erasing previous cultures. The *kapu* system may seem cruel and silly, but its remnants still exist today. For 800 years these new chiefs and their supporters would maintain that they were first. We have seen the evidence left by Hawaii's first people. At one time talk of Earth orbiting the Sun or a changing speed of light was *kapu*. If a theory states that Hawaii was settled after Tahiti, then talk of the earliest Hawaiians is *kapu*.

Though the moieties or Raven and Eagle did not survive in Hawaii, another tradition has become part of our blood. Throughout history, it has become customary for a navigator to take a wife from the place he visits. Chief Nuu found his Lili-noe on Vancouver Island, as evidenced by DNA from the clan of Ina. His descendant Lau Nuu voyaged to America to marry a woman from the Nawao tribe. Even Pili from Samoa took a Hawaiian wife to legitimize his claim to the throne. Many sailors have fallen in love with native women. Through these marriages mitochondrial DNA was spread.

Mauna Kea's summit and its telescopes are described in my previous book THE SPEED OF LIGHT. Some have thought that this mountain is the *Wao Lani* of our ancestors, but we have seen a more likely location in Alaska. Mauna Kea's gentle slopes are not the sharp peaks of *Wao Lani*. Ku of the canoe builders and his wife Lea would not have found any trees atop Mauna Kea.

One site deserves mention, the **Keanokakoi** adze quarry. Atop Mauna Kea's summit glaciers once flowed. Contact between glacial ice and lava forged very hard volcanic rock, excellent for making tools. The importance of the *adze* as a tool is seen on the mountain. This quarry contains many digging sites, most located above the 11,000 foot elevation. The quarry also contains religious shrines, rock shelters, even shell middens. People journeyed great distances to reach this quarry.

The STS-52 flight of *Columbia* in 1992 carried astronaut Charles Lacy Veach, who was raised in Hawaii. He brought into Space an adze from Mauna Kea, which had been a gift from his grandfather. The adze was photographed floating in the Shuttle's flight deck with the Big Island visible in the window. During the flight, Columbia established a communication link with *Hokulea,* which had just left the island of Rarotonga. *Hokulea's* Navigator noted that "*Columbia* is the highest achievement of modern technology today, just as the voyaging canoe was the highest achievement of technology in its day." Like those first Hawaiians, we can follow the whales.

Maui

Near Maui I swam in the surf and shared water with whales. Northeasterly trade winds also strike the island of Maui, making the road to Hana a lush and beautiful path. Gardens and waterfalls grow by the road. The island surrounds the volcanic crater of dormant Mount Haleakala. The southeast region of Maui facing the Big Island is named for Nuu. The Au'Au channel lies between the islands of Maui, Kahoolawe and Lanai. In the Winter I see the same humpback whales we met in Alaska. Humpbacks learned long ago to spend Summer in Alaska and Winter in Hawaii.

Humpbacks come to Hawaii with the same desire as humans, to mate. The clear, warm waters are excellent for males and females to swim and find each other. After mating a humpback gestation period is typically 11-12 months. The timing is right for pregnant females, hungry with two stomachs to feed, to head for Alaska and return to Hawaii the next Winter for birth. No one knows how long the humpbacks have been following this itinerary, for Europeans found Hawaii teeming with whales. The humpbacks have been spawning here a long time.

I am honoured to be good friends with a Hawaiian high chief. He traces his family's lineage back to the island of Maui in the year 427 AD, before islands south of Hawaii were inhabited. On Maui's northwest shore at Makaluapuna Point is the ancient burial site of Honokahua, where graves date back to 610 AD. Hawaiian genealogies say that our islands were settled before arrivals from the South.

Lahaina, once a whaler's base, is now a tourist port where humans board whale-watching cruises. Europeans hunted both humpback and sperm whales. At Ka'anapali Beach we can see another humpback skeleton at the Whalers Museum. Nearby we can also see where Maui the demigod turned a heckler into a stone, a fitting end.

Whale navigation skills easily outdo humans. In their voyages between Alaska and Hawaii humpbacks are never off course by more than one degree! No one knows how they navigate, but it could be due to magnetite, a mineral that exists in some animals. For the Nuu-chah-nulth who followed the whales, they were guides. Whale navigation aid would not be available to sailors from the South, for humpbacks in that hemisphere do not commute across the equator.

Voyagers from the Alaska region also had the aid of the North Star. Honoka'a provides an easy way to measure a canoe's heading and latitude. On clear nights between Alaska and Hawaii it is a constant companion. Sailors in the southern hemisphere would not be familiar with Honoka'a, for it does not appear over their horizon.

My good friends from Alaska once landed in Maui, the eagles! Hawaiian eagles were close relatives of today's white-tailed and bald eagles. Fossils of eagles have been found on three islands. They are thought to have arrived over 100,000 years ago, and for millennia were the biggest land predator of the Islands. Hawaii's eagles are thought to have gone extinct following the arrival of the first Polynesian settlers, before Europeans arrived.

On Maui's southern coast, opposite the Big Island, is mysteriously named **Nuu Landing.** Petroglyphs here mark it as one of the oldest Hawaiian settlements. In the lava are footprints of humans and dogs, said to have been left by Hawaii's first inhabitants. This area, the Kaupo District, was formed by lava from nearby Mount Haleakala. Nuu is vaguely remembered as a spirit dwelling in the hills. Nuu Landing is another likely place he walked.

We can't visit the island of Maui without thinking about the costar of *Moana*. Legends of Maui are told throughout the Pacific. With his fishhook, Maui is said to have pulled giant fish and whole islands from the sea. In some cultures the title of Maui was given to navigators and fishermen. Stories of Maui could describe the exploits of many people. Explorers finding new lands could seemingly "pull islands from the sea".

Over time legends made Maui a trickster, with the powers once given the Raven. He became a shapeshifter who could transform into various animals. Legends about Maui grew--he was responsible for bringing the Sun close to Earth, bringing humans fire, even creating the coconut. In the Philippines he is known as Lumawig, who also voyaged from the East.

Maui was said to be offspring of Ku, who lived in Wao Lani, and the goddess Hina. The youngest of four sons, Maui was said to be born from his mother as an egg. When the egg hatched Maui emerged as a bird with feathers. Only later did he shed his bird feathers to take the shape of a boy. As a shapeshifter Maui most enjoyed becoming a bird.

Moana fans will be pleased to hear that Maui may have been based on a real person. King Wawena, who lived around 680 AD, had four fisherman sons who had the title of Maui. The youngest son, Maui-akalana, would grow to succeed his father as King. In legend Maui created **Iao Needle**. Mark Twain called it "a verdure-clad needle of stone a thousand feet high". As a navigator, the real Maui often visited his Valley Island.

Haleakala

Some stories had Maui living at Kauiki, a hill near **Mount Haleakala**. The enormous crater of this extinct volcano could contain whole cities. The vast slopes of Haleakala, their red volcanic soil littered with rocks, could easily be mistaken for the surface of Mars. From Haleakala's summit we can see Mauna Kea and Kilauea poking above the clouds.

A sunrise seen from atop Haleakala is an unforgettable sight. A sea of billowing clouds gather below the summit. First the warm colours of morning gather over the eastern horizon. Rays of light shoot through the clouds, heralding the morning. Our main event, the Sun appears to rise as Earth turns. Though some speculate that space filled is with dark energies, each morning we are reminded that this is a universe of Light.

Haleakala is said to be site of Maui's battle with the Sun. With his fishhook, Maui captured the Sun until it moved more slowly across the sky. This made the days longer for 6 months of the year. In a Hawaiian chant, "Winter became the Sun's, Summer became Maui's". This story may describe a time when Hawaiian ancestors lived farther north where days were shorter.

Oral histories told many times often confuse east and west. Maui the Navigator can help us here.

East, where the Sun and stars appear to rise over Haleakala, has always been associated with gods and ancestors. West, where the stars disappear, was connected to death and the underworld. Across the Pacific Maui is thought to have sailed from the East. When Hawaiians prayed to the god Ku, who lived in the Wao Lani of ancestors, they always faced toward the rising Sun. In our memories, ancestors of Hawaiians voyaged from the East.

The island of **Kaho'olawe** was the origin point of voyages to Tahiti. The western tip of the island is called Lae-o-Kealaikahiki or "Point on the way to Tahiti." We can hike to this point and see a view of nearby islands. Close by are the remains of a *heiau* where navigators were trained. Rounding this point started navigators on journeys South.

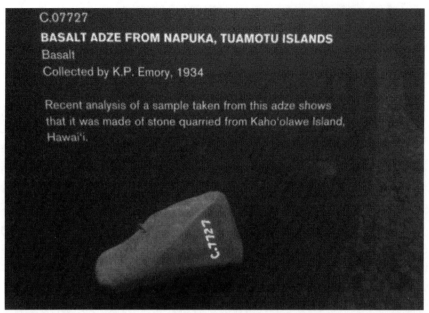

A Hawaiian adze was found in the Tuamoto Islands, more than 2400 miles south of Hawaii, in 1934. It was re-examined during 2007 and found to be made from hawaiite, a rare mineral found in Hawaii. Geologists determined that this adze was mined in Kaho'olawe. Along with the navigation stones, this is rock-hard proof that Hawaiians carrying this *adze* voyaged southward.[lix] In our Hawaiian Islands we have found a centre of Pacific navigation.

Oahu:

Today "the gathering place" is Hawaii's most populous island. On **Waikiki Beach** and the North Shore, Hawaiians follow the waves in our famous sport of surfing. As with canoes, carving surfboards from native trees is an ancient ritual. Some archeological sites date from 4th-5th century. Oahu's windward side contains some of the earliest settlements.

Pearl Harbor, before it became a Naval Base, once really grew pearls. Its many inlets were perfect places for fishponds, where Hawaiians raised oysters and fish. Oahu once contained more fish traps than any other Hawaiian island, but most of these were covered by rising seas and development. The waters surrounding our islands contain many submerged fishponds.

The Navy ships demonstrate that the Hawaiian Islands are, as before, the centre of Pacific navigation. Ships based here have access to the entire ocean. Captain Cook realised on his first visit that Hawaii is a strategic location. Oahu is where *Hokulea* was built and where she returned home in June 2017. From this centre the other Pacific islands are points on the chart.

The Bernice P. Bishop Museum was founded with a goal to find the origins of Polynesians and Hawaiians. The museum contains thousands of artifacts from Pacific islands, though almost nothing from Alaska. The Pakalani Heiau in Waipio Valley was destroyed by fire in 1791, but some of its wood carvings survive in the museum. We can also see sleds from the *Holua* riders of the Big Island. The colourful blankets are made from native *tapa* cloth, which is made by beating tree bark. The museum's planetarium has been used to train navigators of the Polynesian Voyaging Society—I attended the star lessons. A Museum guidebook from 1915 reminds us that Hawaiian canoes were made from American logs. As readers of the introduction know, the story of Hawaii's discovery is in the Bishop Museum's archives.

Lacking the tall trees of Alaska, Hawaiians did not carve tall ancestor poles. They did develop the **Tiki,** wooden carvings devoted to various gods. Legendary *Tiki* was said to be the first man. We can see *Tiki* carvings in museums and gift shops across the islands. Thor Heyerdahl called his ship *Kon Tiki*.

The age of human settlements is a trail in Space and Time. According to the Bishop Museum, today's New Zealand has been settled since about 1200-1300 AD and Tahiti from about 600 AD. If Hawaiian archeological sites date before 300 AD, then the tide of human settlement flowed from the North. Winds and currents from Alaska made that possible. Whales and birds knew this route long ago.

The Koolau Mountains on the windward shore have a primeval beauty, resembling the back of a dinosaur. They have been backdrop of movies like *Jurassic Park* and television shows like *Lost*. Koolau is said to have been originally named for Lua Nuu, who sailed east toward Alaska and became father to the Menehune. Oahu's windward side is also one of the first places voyagers from Alaska would land.

Nu'uanu Pali has spectacular views of both Honolulu and Kaneohe on the windward side. Trade winds blow over Oahu here, making it another windy place. The climactic battle when King Kamehameha conquered Oahu, where Solomon Peleioholani's great grandfather distinguished himself, took place on these cliffs. The battle was fought at close quarters with clubs until the losing side was driven off the cliffs. Like the Nuu-chah-nulth, Hawaiians knew of the bow and arrow but preferred the club as a weapon.

A rock shelter near the Kuli'ou'ou Ridge contained a necklace with a dog's tooth. The islands of the western Pacific had rarely seen dogs. Dogs do not fly, and left no trail between Asia and Hawaii. A voyager from Alaska would proudly wear a dog's tooth as jewelry. Hawaiian dogs may have arrived from the home of Ku, in the North.

Kuka'o'o heiau in Manoa Valley is said to have been built by the Menehune. All Hawaiians have heard of the Menehune, Hawaii's first inhabitants. The name has come to mean "little people," but they may not have been small. The Menehune are known for building large structures, forming lines to pass stones hand-to-hand. As we travel northwest, we find more of their works.

Oahu is the gathering place of not just artifacts but the DNA of peoples. Today's inhabitants are a rainbow from Polynesian islands, Asia, America and elsewhere. Many people have discovered Hawaii, and that is reflected in our genes. The DNA of aboriginal Taiwanese shares gene sequences, numbered 189 217 and 189 217 261, with the Nuu-chah-nulth of

Vancouver Island. Polynesian islanders share these DNA sequences but also have a mutation at Position 247, which first occurred around 1000 BC. DNA allows that Hawaiian natives may also have sailed to other Polynesian islands.

We recall that there is more than one story of the first Hawaiians. One theory says that they travelled through Melanesia and Micronesia, island groups east of the Philippines, before sailing thousands of miles further to the Marquesas Islands and finally Hawaii. On this theory DNA and archeology casts doubt. A genetic study from October 2016 shows that Polynesian ancestors travelled from Asia without stopping at the Melanesian islands in-between.[lx]

Most estimates date settlement of the Marquesas Islands at 400-700 AD or later. The picture in the museum could be upside down—the Marquesas could have been discovered from Hawaii, which was found by voyagers from farther north. Hawaiian navigation stones point to the Marquesas, leaving no doubt that canoes voyaged south. We have seen signs of the first Hawaiians, and temples of the chiefs who pushed them out. Clues to their fate grow on the Garden Island.

Kauai:

Kauai, oldest of the major Hawaiian islands, is also one of the most beautiful. Over 4 million years the high cliffs and valleys have filled with life. Mount Wai'ale'ale funnels moisture from trade winds to its summit. This mountain is the rainiest place on Earth, with an average of 440 inches per year! The rain feeds towering waterfalls that plunge thousands of feet down the cliffs. Our helicopter is but a tiny dot in this overwhelming landscape. When I was a small child my family stayed at Hanalei Bay. Our cottage is in the background of a movie *The Descendants*. This primeval island has also starred in movies about *Blue Hawaii, South Pacific, King Kong* and Jurassic dinosaurs.

On Kauai a descendant of dinosaurs now roams, the **chicken!** Maui calls the movie's *Moana* a princess because she keeps a bird as her animal sidekick. The chicken is thought to have been domesticated in Southeast Asia around 2000 BC, after voyagers had left for Alaska. Along with *Pua'a,* the pig, the chicken is thought to have been introduced to the Polynesian islands via Fiji.

A study from 2016 places the first *Pua'a* on the Hawaiian Islands about 1200 AD, the time when voyagers from southern islands reached Hawaii.[lxi] The chicken is thought to have arrived about the same time. Near the docks of Nawiliwili Harbor we often see a chicken cross the road.

When Spanish arrived in South America in the 16th century, they found that chickens had beaten them there. Why did a chicken cross the Pacific? A 2007 study of chicken bones found in El Arenal, Chile found that they dated before 1400 AD. Their DNA was identical to chickens in Tonga and Samoa. Since chickens can't cross the ocean on their own, their bones are considered proof that Polynesian voyagers brought them to America.[lxii]

On Kauai we hear a unique story, about the invention of the sail. Paka'a was a boy who wished to be a fisherman, but could not row as fast as older boys. Observing the wind's power, he had the idea of capturing it. Paka'a made the first sail out of leaves. On a fishing day he unfurled his sail and easily outraced the stronger rowers. Paka'a became a great sailor without being born a chief or member of his island's upper class.

Off Kauai Captain Vancouver's crew saw a canoe over 60 feet long, the same size as the Haida canoe in today's Museum of Natural History. It was carved from a single giant pine log, before pine trees grew in Hawaii. Hawaiians told Vancouver that the log had drifted from across the sea--they considered it a gift from the gods. Once again a canoe had voyaged from America to Hawaii while still a log.

Kauai also has its own petroglyphs. We can see some examples at Koloa Beach on the island's western side. Like the petroglyphs of Alaska, they face the sea. Archeologists who found them more than a century ago were amazed how similar they were to American petroglyphs. They concluded that Hawaiians and Native Americans must have communicated.[lxiii]

The Wailua River is Hawaii's only river navigable by large boats. The name *Wailua* means "two waters". The river winds by the picturesque **Fern Grotto**. Several important *heiau* are clustered about the river's mouth. **Malae heiau**, just south of the river, is said to have been built and used by the Menehune. On rainy days, the river sometimes washes sand away to reveal petroglyphs. Many of Kauai's petroglyphs are underwater, and are only visible at low tide. In 1848 a native Hawaiian woman reported that they showed a canoe with no outriggers, like an Alaskan canoe. She also saw pictures of an animal as large as a cow, with head and ears like a pig, but no horns. This animal would be unknown to a native Hawaiian but very familiar to Alaskans—a bear.[lxiv] Though Hawaiian petroglyphs may not have arrived from the West, they are reminders of Alaska.

The Alekoko fishpond is a short distance from the cruise ship docks in Nawiliwili Harbor. Its enormous rock wall is over 900 feet long. For those who follow daring archeologists, the fishpond is a location of *Raiders of the Lost Ark*, where Indiana Jones swings on a vine to a waiting seaplane. The natives are understandably upset that Jones steals their artifacts. The fishpond was built by the Menehune.

The Menehune ditch still carries water to taro fields. It is made of stones intricately cut and dressed. The stones fit together so precisely that a knife cannot fit between them. Originally, the ditch was five miles long. It leads to a rock tunnel barely three feet in height. The ditch is evidence of Hawaii's first settlers. Later immigrants piled stones to build temples, but did not cut and dress them.

Hawaiians have long enjoyed eating *poi*. The grey paste is made by pounding the taro root with a stone. In Kauai archeologists have found ring-shaped and D-shaped poi pounders, which are not found elsewhere in Hawaii. There are almost exactly like stone pounders of the Pacific Northwest.

The earliest Hawaiians enjoyed making tools of **hematite**. This hard shiny mineral is an uncommon oxide of iron. It has been identified on Mars, helping to give the planet its reddish colour. A small number of hematite tools and artifacts have been found by archeologists on other Hawaiian islands, nine on the Big Island. The largest number of hematite artifacts, over 400, have been found on Kauai. This is very curious, since Kauai has no known sources of hematite. In 2007 a core made of hematite was found in the Koloa district of Kauai. Analysis of the core by the University of Hawaii at Hilo showed that the hematite came from outside the Hawaiian Islands![lxv] In Alaska hematite is quite common, where it is called "black diamond" and still used for jewellery.

Captain Cook's first landing in Hawaii was at the mouth of the Waimea River. Upriver is spectacular **Waimea Canyon**, "Grand Canyon of the Pacific". Hidden in the valleys and canyons of Kauai are signs of very early settlers. Later immigrants avoided Kauai's interior because they thought the valleys were full of unfriendly spirits. Secrets of the Menehune are hidden in these valleys.

Manini-holo was the chief fisherman of the Menehune. As a small child I explored his cave on Kauai's remote northern shore. The huge cave's dark interior appeared to extend indefinitely. Like the blackness of Space, Earth's interior holds many secrets. I heard the legend that this cave once extended all the way through the island to Waimea Canyon, and was used by the Menehune to escape.

The chiefs who arrived after 1000 AD reduced Hawaii's first inhabitants to "little people," mere subjects. Hawaiian culture was replaced by the *kapu* system. Menehune were pushed out of the other islands to these hidden places. When Kauai's king took a census in 1800, 65 people from the town of Wainiha claimed their nationality as "Menehune". That was the last official count, but today some in Kauai claim to be descended from the Menehune.

The spectacular Na Pali Coast contains valleys completely inaccessible from land, a romantic place to get away for it all. **Honopu Valley** is known as "Valley of the Lost Tribe" because of stories that an ancient people once lived there.

The Hawaiian Islands also had an "untouchable" caste called the *kauwa*, who some historians think were remnants of the Menehune.[lxvi] Little is told about the origins of the *kauwa*. They were treated poorly, kept as slaves and often used for human sacrifice. They were not allowed to have any contact with the ruling classes. The *kauwa* disappeared around the beginning of the 19th century, along with the Menehune.

Nihoa, Northwest of Kauai, is a small island with barely enough land to feed 100 people. Despite the island's small size, archeologists have found signs that people lived and grew crops here. Adzes found on Nihoa are almost exactly like 5th century adzes from Molokai. Refugees from the other Hawaiian Islands may have lived here.

On Mokumanamana, today called Necker Island, stone figures were found that were unlike any in the other Islands.^{lxvii} Standing stones and *heiau* here point toward the stars. Every stone on Necker is astronomical, for the island sits on the Tropic of Cancer, farthest latitude north where the Sun passes directly overhead. In Kauai's history the Menehune were driven out of the other islands until Nihoa and Necker were their only refuge. In some stories, the Menehune sailed away as far as today's New Zealand.

On our Hawaiian Islands we have seen signs of settlers starting from the time of Chief Nuu. Currents and winds, the paths of whales and birds, could have brought them from Alaska and British Columbia. They may have been the people remembered as the Menehune, the first Hawaiians. As to whether Hawaii was discovered from the North or the South, both theories could be right. Different peoples have discovered Hawaii at different times.

During 1987 *Hokulea* attempted to sail from the Marquesas Islands to test the theory that early Hawaiians came that way. This would involve sailing both North and West, maintaining a precise course in uncooperative currents. Despite its crew of brave sailors and navigators, *Hokulea* couldn't make it. Opposing winds made the passage from the Marquesas too difficult.

For discovering Hawaiian Islands, canoes carved in Alaska and the Pacific Northwest have an enormous advantage. Like Viking longboats, they are designed to be rowed. As Vikings independently learned, warriors with strong arms can also row. Double canoes, and even Captain Cook's big ships, were at the mercy of fickle winds. Aside from providing an upper-body workout, rowing allows us to make headway even when there is no wind.

The Polynesian Voyaging Society wished their next canoe to be built of native materials like *Koa* wood. During 1989 and 1990 their navigators searched the hills of four Hawaiian Islands, but could not find a big enough *Koa* tree. Here the Whale House of the Chilkat returns to our story. Herb Kane, the artist/designer of *Hokulea*, introduced the Society's best Navigator to a senior Tlingit from the town of Klukwan. In the Whale House, this man was known as "Big Fin". The Tlingit offered to give the Hawaiians two logs of their choosing, and invited the Navigator to see Alaska.

Arriving in Ketchikan, the Navigator was given a tour on a DeHavilland Twin Otter seaplane. Having flown in the copilot's seat of a Twin Otter, I can attest to what he saw. A native Hawaiian, the Navigator had never imagined forests like these. Thousands upon thousands of square miles were filled with huge trees. The Tlingit had already found two spruce trees 220 feet tall, perfect for the twin hulls of a canoe. The navigator felt that Alaska was "spiritual," a place of rejuvenation. The navigator did some soul-searching, for he had hoped to build the canoe from Hawaiian logs. He consulted supporters at the Bishop Museum and family members. Finally an agreement was made for the Alaskans to make a gift of the two trees. They were cut down in a ceremony attended by both Hawaiians and Alaskans. As is custom, the trees were named before being harvested. This canoe's first name was Tlingit, *Khutxh ayun nah Ha Kayatun,* or "Steering by the Stars". She was renamed *Hawai'iloa*.

In 1995 *Hokulea*, along with *Hawai'iloa* and four canoes built on other islands, tried to sail from Tahiti to Hawaii via the Marquesas Islands. Entering the "doldrums" near the equator, where lack of winds can leave a ship becalmed, all the canoes save for *Hokulea* had to use engines or be towed. *Hokulea* herself was towed from Tahiti to the Marquesas. Though these canoes used traditional navigation, they knew of Hawaii's existence and where our Islands could be found. They reached the latitude of Hawaii and then sailed west, knowing that islands were there. For early navigators finding Hawaii from the South would have been extremely difficult.

After reaching Honolulu in 1995, *Hawai'iloa* toured Alaska and the Pacific Northwest while *Hokulea* toured California. The canoes didn't sail to America, but were carried on big cargo ships. The voyage was also thanks for the gift of two Alaskan logs. Stopping in many Alaskan ports, *Hawai'iloa* emphasised the many connections between Alaska and Hawaii. In 1999 *Hokulea* sailed from Hawaii to the Marquesas Islands, but not in the other direction. During her round-the-world voyage, *Hokulea* sailed from the Marquesas to Hawaii only by detouring to Tahiti. Though sailing from the Marquesas is difficult, canoes from America have reached Hawaii multiple times.

My travels between Hawaii and Alaska have given me new appreciation of our Islands. Many Hawaiians will be surprised to hear that some of their forebears may have come from Alaska, but the area that Pacific voyagers explored is now doubled. Not only did people have the ability to sail from America to Hawaii, but they also sailed back. We have seen signs of the earliest Hawaiians, and navigational stones pointing the way south. If Hawaii was settled in ancient times, the tide of exploration would have travelled this way. The earliest Hawaiians are remembered today as the Menehune. Centuries ago voyaging ceased and the homeland was forgotten— we must travel to Tahiti to find out why. Hawaii would be discovered again by a navigator from the island called England.

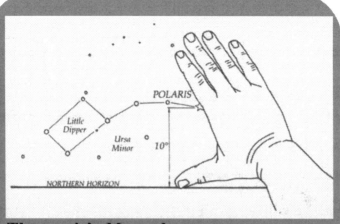

The movie's *Moana* learns to measure the altitude of stars with her hand. When your hand is outstretched with the thumb lying on the horizon, the knuckle of your first finger is 10 degrees away. The top of your oustretched fingers is 20 degrees away. This works even for small people. A navigator near Orchid Island would use Hokopa'a to measure latitude as 22 degrees North. This is also the latitude of the Hawaiian Islands.

TAHITI

DISTANT LAND

August 12, 2018 AD

The year 2018 AD is a worldwide anniversary. From Yorkshire to Australia and across the Pacific we remember a sailing 250 years ago. On this day in 1768 His Majesty's Barque *Endeavour* set sail from Plymouth, England. Not a warship or ship of the line, this little bark was originally built and used to carry coal. Her new captain was a diamond who also came from coal. He was James Cook of the Royal Navy, one of the greatest navigators of all time.

Centuries after Polynesian voyages slowed, European explorers appeared in the Pacific. With their written language brought from the Mediterranean, they left us detailed records of voyages and dates. With the astronomical knowledge of Europe, James Cook explored and charted the Pacific. None of the other voyages described here detracts from Captain Cook's achievements. On three great voyages of exploration he sailed from England to Australia and around the world, ventured into both the Antarctic and the Arctic, charted many islands, journeyed to Alaska and discovered Hawaii for the Europeans. Without being born a chief or a member of his nation's upper class, Cook explored all these places in a single lifetime.[lxviii]

In hopes of following James Cook's path, I boarded a new *Endeavour*. The sailing replica built in 1995 contains a mast block from Cook's original ship. In the hold an extra deck was built for the officer's quarters. The first thing I noticed is that the overhead or ceiling is low, barely five feet! For Cook, who stood well over six feet tall, the quarters were a tight fit. This new ship has toured the world as a reminder of Cook's voyages.

I've seen another new *Endeavour,* the space shuttle displayed in Los Angeles. Nearly all who dream of the sea and stars, even space shuttle astronauts, feel humbled by James Cook. Though our spacecraft make circles around the Earth, Cook found unknown new lands. He made accurate charts covering most of the Pacific. His achievements seem so monumental that we wonder how we can even approach them. I would discover an opportunity in the light of the stars.

James Cook first saw light on November 7, 1728 in the village of Marton, Yorkshire. His name appears in the records of St. Cuthbert's Church. In 1978, for his 250th birthday, the Captain Cook Birthplace Museum opened in Marton. A vase to the south of the museum marks his birthplace.

Cook was the son of a Scottish farm labourer in Great Ayton. Today the stone cottage of the Cook family has voyaged to a park in Melbourne, Australia. The Cooks were not sailors, and young James' future seemed to offer little beyond the farm.

At the age of seventeen James was apprenticed to a shopkeeper in the fishing village of Staithes. The Captain Cook and Staithes Heritage Centre contains a replica of the little shop. The port of Whitby was then a centre of the growing coal trade, a harbour for ships filled with the black stuff. The sight and smell of the ocean entered the shop windows. After 18 months working in retail, James signed on as a deckhand on a coal ship.

The 1740's were near the start of the Industrial Revolution. The black coal that fueled this revolution was carried down England's coasts in stout, roomy ships with flat bottoms. The rough North Sea has always been unforgiving to sailors. Barefoot young men climbed rope ladders to work sails. Constant work with ropes wore on their hands. Men turned wooden capstans to haul up anchors. The winds were cold and unpredictable. Rocks and shoals threatened a ship with destruction. Within a coal ship the black dust floated everywhere and stuck to everything. This hard routine was excellent training for a life at sea.

Cook was intelligent, studious, a hard worker and a commanding figure. In the attic of the house where he lived while an apprentice, he studied mathematics by candlelight. The house is now the **Captain Cook Memorial Museum** in Whitby.

James advanced rapidly in the merchant marine. At age 29 he was offered command of a ship. Surprisingly, he turned down command to enter the Royal Navy as an able seaman. Cook had always had a desire to join the Navy. By the 1750's Britain's maritime empire was expanding. A looming conflict with France would become the Seven Years War. The Navy offered a chance to be part of something greater, and adventure in faraway lands.

The war from 1756 to 1763 pitted Britain and France in a battle for American colonies. James Cook took part in the capture of one French warship and the sinking of another. During 1758, he helped in the capture of the Fortress of Louisburg and the siege of Quebec City. Cook's talents for mapping and surveying were invaluable to the Navy. Working from a small boat, sometimes beneath French guns, he charted the Saint Lawrence River and the approaches to Quebec City. Cook's work was instrumental in capture of the city, the Battle for the Plains of Abraham, and British victory in the war.

In the closing days of 1762, Cook found time to marry Elizabeth Batts, daughter of an innkeeper in London. It was a rapidly growing city with three quarters of a million people. The streets were crowded with people and horses, the skies marred by smoke from coal plants. After all his voyages but one, Cook would return to Elizabeth and their children in a house on Mile End Road. I have searched Mile End Road for signs of James and Elizabeth Cook's house, but it no longer survives.

Returning to America after the war's end, Cook took the job of surveying the coast of Newfoundland. From 1763 to 1767 he did painstaking work sounding and drawing charts from a small boat. Cook's charts of Newfoundland were so accurate that they were used into the 20th century. In 1766 he saw and reported a solar eclipse. Though Cook was still officially an enlisted man, his talent and hard work brought him attention from Britain's Admiralty.

250 years ago half of Earth was unknown to Europeans. Polynesian long-distance voyaging had ceased, though the First Peoples of the Pacific Northwest still maintained the tradition. Only a few scattered islands had been seen by Europeans. Most of the Pacific had not been crossed by their ships, and was full of uncharted lands.

Aristotle of Athens, who gathered evidence that Earth was spherical, thought that a southern continent was needed to balance the land masses in the North. Ptolemy, Librarian of Alexandria in the 2nd century AD, postulated that Earth was centre of the universe and contained an unknown southern land. We visited their homes in my book THE SPEED OF LIGHT. Maps in the 1760's showed a continent called *Terra Australis Incognita*. European navigators before Cook had vainly searched for this legendary land.

Abel Tasman was also born to humble beginnings, in a small North Holland village in 1603. Early in life he distinguished himself by learning to read and write, very important skills. At 30, about the age James Cook joined the Royal Navy, Tasman signed up with the Dutch East India Company. Within a year he was appointed captain of a ship. During 1636 Tasman was second-in-command of an exploration voyage East of Japan. Tasman's talent and hard work brought him attention from the East India Company.

Tasman's own first voyage of exploration set out from the port of Batavia on August 14, 1642 with two ships. The East India Company hoped to find *Terra Australis* and claim it for the Dutch. Tasman stopped at Mauritius in the Indian Ocean, and then sailed past 49 degrees south. There his ships found the heavy seas, hail, and fog of the "roaring forties". Returning to 44 degrees South, Tasman sailed east still searching for a southern continent. He missed the coast of Australia, but sighted an island on November 24. Tasman named his discovery Van Dieman's Land for the Governor of Batavia. Today we call it Tasmania.

Sailing farther East, Tasman discovered the islands he named New Zealand. Awestruck, the crews of his ships saw high mountains piercing the clouds. They followed this coast north until they rounded a cape and saw open water to the east. They anchored in a bay where canoes full of warriors ventured from shore. The first encounter between Europeans and the Maori turned into a deadly attack. Prevented from landing, Tasman named the place

Murderers Bay and continued north. Had he explored deeper into the Bay, he would have found the strait between the North and South Islands. At the Three Kings Islands, the crew had another unfriendly encounter with local Maori. Returning to Batavia, he discovered the islands of Tonga and Fiji, where he nearly collided with Fiji's Nanuku Reef. Tasman's crew left the place they called New Zealand without landing.

Tasman's second voyage in February 1644 explored the North coast of Australia. He discovered more new islands, but missed the Strait between Australia and New Guinea. The strait was discovered by Spanish Captain Luis Torres in 1606, but was kept a secret. The Dutch East India Company thought Tasman's discoveries unimportant, for he did not find gold or the legendary *Terra Australis*. No one knew if his New Zealand was part of a continent. Only later did others realise the value of Abel Tasman's discoveries.

For April 1769, astronomers predicted a transit of Venus, when the planet would cross directly in front of the Sun. In the 1760's the size of our solar system was unknown. Observations showed that Jupiter was five times Earth's distance from the Sun, but the length of this *astronomical unit* was unknown. For this reason Ole Roemer's first estimate of THE SPEED OF LIGHT, found from Jupiter's moons, could not be completely accurate. If astronomers could measure the speed of Venus, which orbits at about 0.67 astronomical units, they could use Newton's Laws to calculate the solar system's size. Transits of Venus happen on average every 120 years. The Royal Society of London, a group of Naturalists, hoped to see the transit from a distant land.

Captain James Wallis of *HMS Dolphin* found Tahiti on June 18, 1767. Finding the Tahitians friendly, Wallis stayed a month before returning to England. *HMS Dolphin* carried a ship's goat, the first farm animal to sail around the world. The goat would also accompany James Cook, giving it the chance to orbit Earth a second time.

Captain Louis-Antoine de Bougainville of the French ship *Boudeuse* was distinguished as both a mathematician and a soldier. Following in Wallis' wake, Bougainville found Tahiti on April 2, 1768. His French crew spread tales of the island paradise, of beautiful beaches and dark-haired women. De Bougainville would continue exploring westward until turned by Australia's Great Barrier Reef. During the next century nearly every Pacific voyage would stop at Tahiti. Britain and France both desired a piece of paradise, an excellent place to view the transit of Venus.

Endeavour

At age 39 James Cook was a master mariner who had commanded small ships, but still officially an enlisted man. The ranks of Navy officers were filled by the chiefs of Britain's upper classes. The Royal Society wanted a ship to observe Venus, and the Navy agreed to provide one. To command the voyage, the Admiralty selected James Cook. With his experience, from North Sea colliers to mapping Newfoundland, Cook was the perfect choice. His new responsibilities led to a commission as Lieutenant Cook of the Royal Navy.

The ship chosen for the voyage seemed as unlikely as her commander. She began life as the *Earl of Pembroke*, carrying coal in the North Sea. Unlike the fast warships of the Royal Navy, she had a stout hull and a flat bottom. Her hull could carry lots of cargo for a long voyage, and also could be beached in an emergency. Independently the Nuu-chah-nulth had discovered the advantages of a flat bottom. During April 1768 the coal ship was admitted to the Royal Dockyard in East London, to be reborn as *Endeavour*.

Since the Bible and Noah, Europeans had learned to build ships from wooden planks. Trees were milled into planks with axes and tools of iron. The spaces between planks were filled with pitch or caulk. To keep a hollow ship from tipping over, the bottoms were filled with heavy ballast. Planks allowed wooden ships to be built large, but continually suffered from leaks. Europeans, along with Polynesians of the catamaran, could not fathom how Native Americans could cross the Pacific in a canoe carved from a single log.

Because of his stellar performance in navigation and observing an eclipse, Cook was the voyage's official astronomer. His official mission was to observe the transit. The Naturalist of the voyage was **Joseph Banks** of the Royal Society. Banks, 25 years old, came from a wealthy family and had an insatiable curiosity about nature. He had independently traveled to Newfoundland observing plants and animals. On *Endeavour's* voyage he brought another astronomer, two artists, two botanists, and four servants. Banks was painted with an *adze* at his feet. He saw the voyage as a thrilling adventure, though one from which they might not return. *Endeavour* also had had had a secret mission, which Cook carried in sealed orders.

Joseph Banks, a man of science, would gain renown as a Naturalist. In 1768 my NASA Johnson Space Center job title "Scientist" had not been invented. That word would be first used in the 1830's to describe a woman named Mary Sommerville. She was a polymath, learned in many scientific fields. "Man of science" was inappropriate for Mary, so a woman was first to be called Scientist.

James Cook would be renowned for keeping his crews healthy. Until the 18th century the disease scurvy meant death for sailors. Today we know that scurvy is caused by a lack of Vitamin C, which the human body can store for no more than 6 weeks. Bringing supplies of sauerkraut and onions, Cook insisted that his crew eat their vegetables. He ordered that the crew wash regularly and keep their quarters clean, unusual habits for 18th century European sailors. During the voyage Cook's crew lost not a single man to scurvy.

Endeavour departed England on August 27, 1768. During the voyage Naturalist Banks thrilled in the flora and fauna. On a calm day the ship's rigging became covered in butterflies, which Banks sent his servants to collect. While the ship was anchored outside Rio de Janeiro, Banks and an artist slipped ashore to collect plants. On another day the ship was swarmed by flying fish, which landed on the deck to become dinner. Sailing around the rough seas of Cape Horn, *Endeavour* proved herself more than seaworthy. On April 13, 1769 the ship dropped anchor in Matavai Bay, Tahiti.

The name Tahiti comes from the Proto-Polynesian word *Tafiti,* meaning "distant land". Movie fans remember "Tefiti" as the distant land *Moana* must sail to. Some have thought that Tahiti and the Polynesian homeland of Hawai'i are the same, but they are very different names for different islands. The voyagers who named Tahiti must have sailed from a distant homeland.

French Polynesia consists of five island groups. The Society Islands, named by James Cook after the Royal Society, include the Windward islands of Tahiti and Moorea. The Leeward Islands include Raiatea, Huahine, and Bora Bora. The Tuamoto Islands include Napuka, where a stone adze from Hawaii was found. Other island groups in French Polynesia are the Gambier and Austral Islands. The Marquesas, nearest French Polynesian islands, are about 2,200 miles from Hawaii.

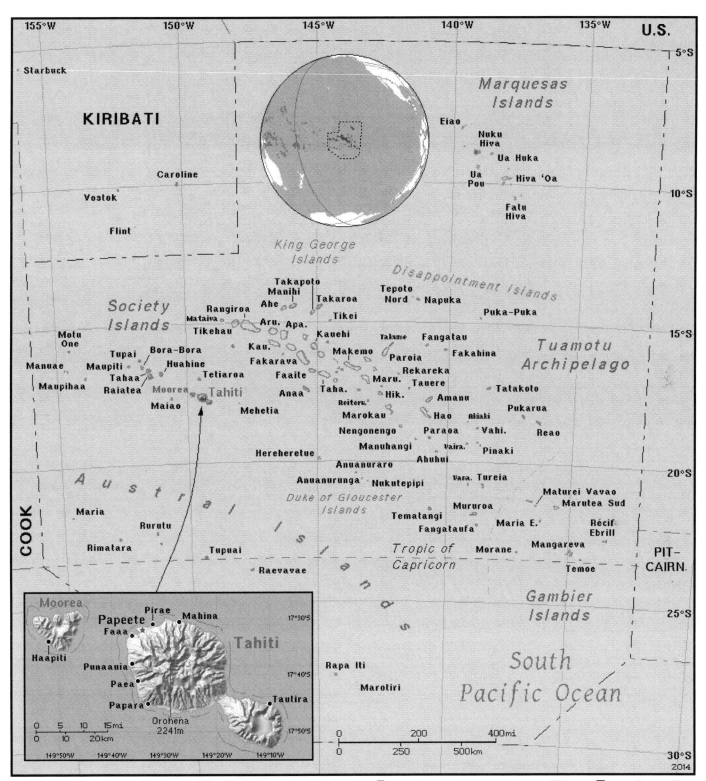

FRENCH POLYNESIA

Tahiti is another young island, formed as a volcano between 1.4 million and 870,000 years ago. Like Hawaii, Tahiti sits atop a hot spot rising up from Earth's interior. The northwest portion of the island, Tahiti Nui rose first, followed by smaller Tahiti Iti. After rising, the volcano of Tahiti Nui collapsed, leaving great gouges in the island's flanks. Erosion from the heavy tropical rains carved deep valleys which filled with life. The islands are surrounded by a garden of coral reefs.

Papeete the capitol was once a whaler's port. From July to October we can see humpback whales near Tahiti and Moorea. They are not the same whales we saw in Alaska and Hawaii, for these humpbacks spend the southern Summer in the Antarctic. Manta rays can be encountered in a lagoon called La Ferme aux Mantas (Manta farm) on the atoll of Tikehau. The Golden Plovers in Tahiti *are* the same birds we saw in Alaska, for they do pass the equator on their nonstop flights. Possibly birds were a clue for Tahitian navigators, but following the Plovers would take them straight to Alaska. Sailors following the whales would end up in Antarctica.

The first humans in Tahiti were a people called Manahune, which became the Tahitian word for "commoner". At one time the island was called Tahiti-manahune. These early inhabitants were also displaced by chiefs from Raiatea.[lxix] The temples of these early Tahitians can still be found in the island's interior. Common names and temples suggest that these first Tahitians were related to Hawaii's Menehune.

Hawaiian oral history tells of early voyages to the Society Islands. King Kalakaua's telling starts in Waipio Valley where Chief Mo'ikeha, his brother and his wife lived until flooding forced them to leave. This is thought to have happened around the 11th century AD. Waipio Valley is exposed to the ocean, having suffered floods as recently as 1946 and 1977 AD. Mo'ikeha is said to have landed at the island of Raiatea, which would later become another centre of navigation.

Marae are temples for rituals and sacrifice. After the 11th century the Tahitian islands would taken over by chiefs from Raiatea. On the Tahitian coast the new rulers built *marae* larger than the earlier temples in the island's interior. Led by the priest Pa'ao these chiefs sailed to Hawaii and built their temples atop the old Hawaiian *heiau*, as we saw at Mo'okini. These new temples had walls to keep the "commoners" outside. Today we can freely visit *marae* on the Tahitian islands. **Arahurahu marae** on Tahiti's southwestern side, is one of the most beautiful *marae* on the island. Two newly carved stone *Tiki* guard the entrance. Nearby we can see a pen where pigs waited for sacrifice. Arahurahu is one of the few *marae* to have been restored, and is still used for ceremonies today.

Mahaiatea marae was, at the time of Captain Cook's first visit, the grandest on Tahiti. The platform was 250 feet long and over 40 feet high. Today the ruins, east of the village of Papara, are barely visible in a parking lot. A priest named Tupaia, who would join Cook aboard Endeavour, supervised the *marae's* construction.

Maere nuutere is in Tahiti's interior, only rarely visited today. It consists of a simple platform, typical of the *marae* built by Tahiti's first inhabitants. These inland temples resemble the *heiau* of Necker Island and the earliest Hawaiians. Chiefs from Raiatea would build larger *marae* with walls, overshadowing the temples of the "little people".[lxx]

Maiva village on the island of Huahine was once a home of these kings and aristocrats. Near Maiva they built more than 30 different *marae*, which can be seen on a hike up Matairea Hill. The waters surrounding Huahine contain stone fishtraps similar to those in Hawaii and British Columbia. Matairea marae was the most important on Huahine.

The grounds of the Hotel Bali Hai on Huahine contain the oldest archeological site in the Society Islands. Among its treasures were whalebone pendants and parts of a canoe. The site has been dated to about 850 AD. On Hawaii we have found sites dated much earlier, indicating that the Hawaiian Islands were settled first.

Raiatea, second largest island in French Polynesia, is today largely unspoiled by development. Raiatea and the adjacent island of Tahaa are encircled by a single coral reef; they may have once been a single island. We can go diving on the reef or take a boat to the Anapa pearl farm, built on stilts over the water. Enjoying unspoiled Raiatea, we can hardly tell that it was a centre of navigation and religion.

Taputapuatea marae on Raiatea was once the religious centre of the Pacific. Situated on the coast facing the reef entrance, it holds the secret to why voyaging stopped. The *marae* trained navigators who spread their religion as far as Hawaii. Visitors arrived at *Marae Hauviri* on the waterfront. At the platform of *Marae Oputeina*, they would say farewells. Departing chiefs took souvenir stones from Taputapuatea to *marae* all over Pacific. On Oahu's coast, a satellite temple was named Kapukapuatea.

After the priest Pa'ao took his religion to Hawaii, Taputapuatea was itself taken over by the deadly cult of Oro. The cult had an insatiable appetite for human sacrifice. The name Taputapuatea would mean "sacrifice from abroad". Each year canoes from other islands ritually sailed into the reef entrance bringing human tribute for the cult.

The cult of Oro spread until a high priest from Rarotonga was murdered, then another priest was killed in revenge. For centuries the Maori remembered the priest's death and the others killed at the *marae*. The deaths led to a *kapu* on canoes sailing to Taputapuatea. For centuries the Maori would be suspicious of outsiders bringing strange religions, explaining the hot welcome they gave to Abel Tasman. Voyaging from distant islands ceased.

In the 14th century one last canoe full of settlers was sent out from Raiatea with a vow that the island would be *kapu* until the settlers or their descendants returned. The canoe headed for Hawaii but was never heard from again. With the end of voyaging, the navigational knowledge taught at Taputapuatea was lost. This little-known story was told to the crew of *Hokulea* arriving here in 1985, in hope that the *kapu* had finally ended. Though the long-distance voyages of Polynesians stopped, Northwest tribes like the Haida and Tlingit maintained the tradition.

Arriving in Tahiti and knowing none of its history, Cook's crew saw Tahiti as paradise. The sailors were wide-eyed upon seeing dark-haired women walking and paddling canoes bare-breasted. To Naturalist Joseph Banks the Tahitian Islands were a paradise of plant specimens. Later Banks would recommend Tahitian breadfruit trees as a food supply.

In the depths of Maraa Grotto the crew found fresh water. The grotto, curtained by ferns, seems like a magical place. Centuries later the artist Paul Gauguin would be inspired by a swim here. Many travelers would be hypnotised by the paradise of Tahiti.

At **Point Venus** the crew built a fort to observe the transit. Today the fort is gone, but we can still visit the black sand beach. William Hodges, the expedition artist, sketched the view from One Tree Hill. Today the one tree is also gone, but we can still enjoy the spectacular view. On June 3, 1769, a day when the temperature passed 100 degrees Fahrenheit, the eclipse happened on schedule. Cook's sketch of the eclipse survives today.

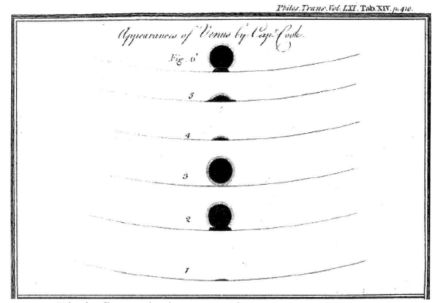

Their first mission complete, James Cook opened his sealed orders. *Endeavour* was to venture southward, find *Terra Australis*, and claim it for Britain. If they didn't find it, they would find and claim Tasman's New Zealand.[lxxi] Upon hearing this new mission, Joseph Banks and the crew were thrilled. It would be a naturalist's dream, the adventure of a lifetime. Cook himself wished to go farther than anyone had gone, as far as it was possible to go.

Before leaving Tahiti, *Endeavour* picked up a local guide named Tupaia. His knowledge of navigation amazed even Cook. Wherever *Endeavour* voyaged in the Pacific, Tupaia could always point the way back to Tahiti. He was born on Raiatea, and had been a priest at Taputapuatea until its wars forced him to flee. In Tahiti, he became both a close advisor to the High Chief and lover to the High Chief's wife! He supervised construction of the big *marae* at Mahaiatea. Tupaia was learned in astronomy, navigation and geography. He could draw a chart of the Pacific from Fiji to the Marquesas, but had been to only a few of those islands. During Tupaia's lifetime the range of voyaging had shrunk to a few islands of eastern Polynesia. Along with Cook's crew, Tupaia would see lands he had only dreamed of.

Tahitians and British alike were sad to see *Endeavour* leave paradise. As Cook prepared to sail, two crewmembers jumped ship and ran into the forest with Tahitian women. The sailing was delayed while they were rounded up. This would not be the last mutiny in Tahiti. Leaving the islands on July 13, Endeavour sailed to 40 degrees south and the rough seas of the "Roaring Forties".

Among the lands on Tupaia's chart was a place that held secrets of Polynesian origins, islands that Cook wouldn't find until another voyage. These were the islands of Tonga and Fiji that Abel Tasman had previously encountered. They spawned another culture that voyaged to Hawaii. Important to movie fans, they were the home of *Moana!*

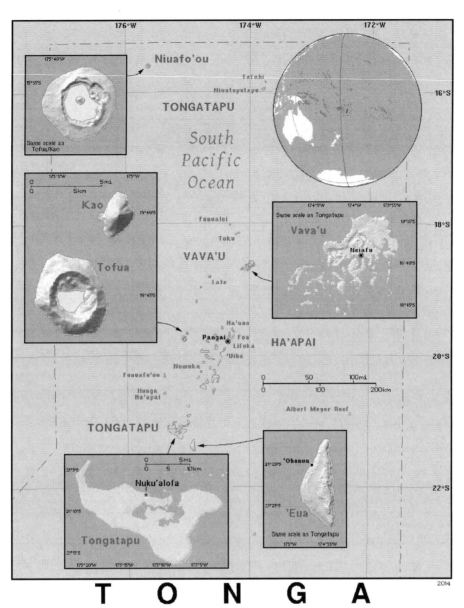

T O N G A

The archipelago of **Tonga** was first settled about 800 BC. Archeologists have determined this from a pottery style called Lapita that spread in the Pacific. We know very little about who spread the pottery, whether it represents an unknown culture or a very good pottery salesman. The name Lapita is not native, but from diggers who named "La pit" where it was found.

This smaller Polynesian Triangle of Tonga, Samoa and Fiji would form the Tonga Maritime Chiefdom, a trading empire that began around 950 AD. The Maritime Chiefdom began on the island of Tongatapu, "Sacred Tonga". Legends of the demigod Maui have travelled here too. On Tongatapu we can see the huge gateway called **Ha'amonga 'a Maui** or "Maui's yoke". This gate or *Trilithon* is made from 3 slabs of coral limestone, each weighing 30-40 tons! The *trilithon* is often compared to England's Stonehenge. Notches in the stones may indicate solstices and equinoxes. In legends it was built by Maui from stones carried in a canoe from Wallis Island 510 miles away.

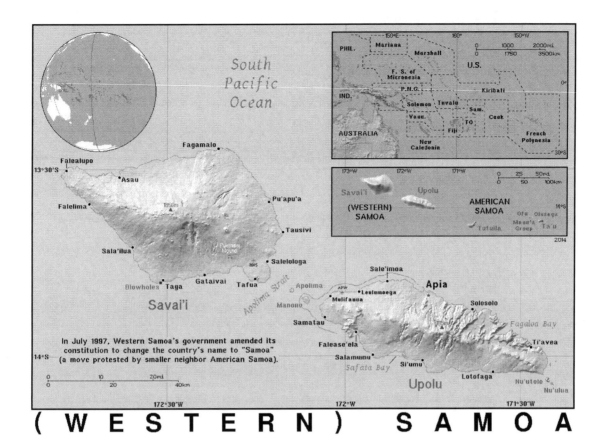

(W E S T E R N) S A M O A

The islands of **Western Samoa** are located about 500 miles north-northeast from Tongatapu, and Fiji is 400 miles west-northwest. The early "Lapita" pottery spread here from the West but no farther. Early inhabitants of Hawaii and Tahiti did not use pottery, instead making bowls from wood. Water was carried in the bottle gourd, a plant that grew in South America 10,000 years ago. The bottle gourd is one more clue that humans carried it from America.

The movie *Moana* takes place on the fictional island of Moto Nui. The filmmakers were thoughtful to fill her island with chickens and *Pua'a* the **pig**. This *Pua'a* was photographed in Samoa.

Early settlers of the Tonga region brought these farm animals from Southeast Asia, but not the dog. The early "Lapita" sites in Tonga, Fiji and Samoa contain no signs of dogs. Even when Europeans arrived in the 17th century, no dogs were found. In Alaska and Hawaii dogs were always part of the family. People of the Marquesas and Society Islands, said to have been found by Hawai'iloa and his brothers, brought dogs to the first settlements. As the pig was brought from the West, paths of dogs show early migration southward.

The giant canoes of legend, used by Maui to build the Triathlon, really existed. The movie's *Moana* finds one hidden in a cave, and by playing its drums discovers her voyaging heritage. This canoe originated in the islands of Fiji.

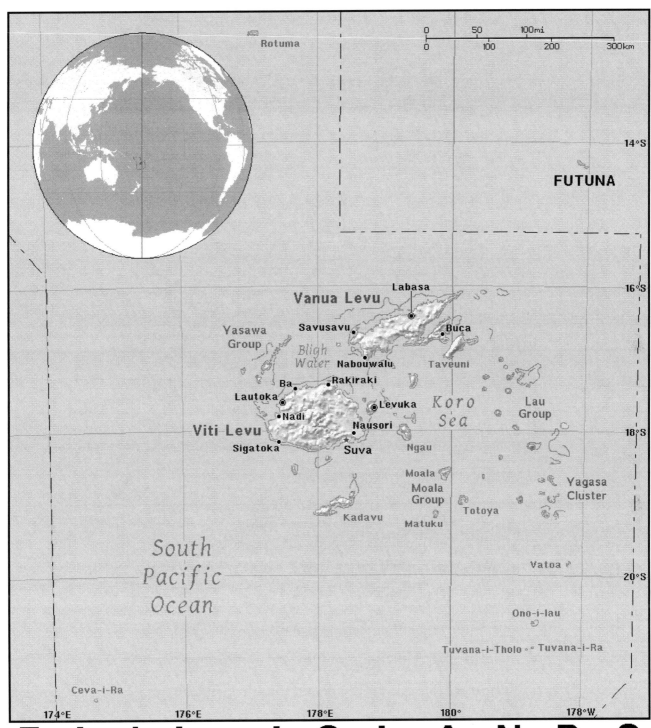

Like someone exploring Cook's *Endeavour*, *Moana* is in awe of her voyaging ancestors. Later a ghostly navigator in the canoe, the James Cook of another time, salutes *Moana* before unfurling an enormous sail and speeding off. His vessel is a **Drua,** one of the greatest vessels of the ocean. One of these "battleships of the Pacific" was measured at 118 feet long, longer than Cook's *Endeavour*, long as a Space Shuttle orbiter! A steering oar in the Fiji Museum is 33 feet long. Propelled by enormous sails made of woven *pandanus* leaves, the *drua* could travel at speeds of 15 knots, faster than *Endeavour*.

The **Drua** could carry crews of 200 warriors to nearby islands, or a payload of over 30 tons. This was the solution to how the giant limestone pieces of Ha'amonga 'a Maui were transported. Like the Space Shuttle, the *drua* could carry big building blocks. In Samoa the canoes were called *alia* and in Tonga *kalia*

Fijians say their culture began on the remote Norokorokoyamas, "Sacred Islands" near Viti Levu. Polynesians belong to the Clan of Ina, with DNA sequences 189 217 and 189 217 261. Sometime around 1000 BC near Fiji a mutation at position 247 appeared. This sequence 189 217 247 261 is called the Polynesian motif, which traveled as far as Hawaii.

On Tahiti and the Society Islands are clues that voyagers from the North reached here long ago. Their temples are hidden in Tahiti's interior. On the island of Raiatea the great *marae* at Taputapuatea was another centre of voyaging, which also holds the secret to why voyages stopped. The islands of Tonga, Fiji and Samoa show signs of the distinct Polynesian culture, and giant oceangoing canoes. I would find more clues in a land of a white clouds, final destination of voyagers from the homeland.

I have had the good fortune to earn a living both as a Naturalist and a Scientist at NASA. In following the trail of Naturalists like John Muir and Joseph Banks, I was struck by the reputation of today's scientists. As the word was coined to describe Mary Sommerville in the 1830's, in 1823 another young woman named Mary Shelley wrote *Frankenstein*, the archetypal novel of the misguided scientist. Since then literature, and in turn movies and television, have been filled with mad scientists and evil scientists. The Naturalist, in contrast, enjoys a proud reputation earned by working with Nature. Today some scientists have forgotten Nature and chosen another path.

That led to darkness larger than *Moana* faced.

The Southern Cross was known by Ptolemy of Alexandria's library, but forgotten by Europeans until they voyaged South in the 16th century. As the North Star is in Alaska's flag, *Crux* is part of flags from Australia, Brazil, New Zealand, Papua New Guinea and Samoa. The top and bottom stars of the Southern Cross are six degrees apart. When the distance between them is equal to the lower star's distance from the horizon, we are at 21 degrees North, the latitude of Honolulu or the islands of Taiwan.

NEW ZEALAND

February 6, 2010

Thousands gathered at the Waitangi Treaty Grounds to see the canoe's first launch. Christened *Matawhaorua* after the first ship to discover the island, the canoe was 114 feet long with a crew of over 120 rowers. Following tradition, the canoe was decorated in red, white and black. The figurehead was a warrior tattooed in red and black. A fleet of 22 canoes escorted *Matawhaorua* into the ocean. That day the Maori remembered their voyaging heritage.

That same day a heritage was abandoned.

On the far side of the world in Houston we worked in laboratories and on computers. We had a Vision to send humans to the Moon, as our ancestors had done just two generations before. For weeks rumours had swirled through our NASA offices that change was coming. On the first week of February 2010 the new budget officially ended our mission to the Moon.

On February 8 at Johnson Space Center, I went to a meeting with the new NASA administrator. The other attendees, the most qualified engineers and scientists, were angry and frustrated. All our lives we had dreamed of the Moon. One woman, whose job was to design a new lunar lander, was in tears. Within a few months, thousands of NASA rowers would be out of work.

The *Matawhaorua* canoe is launched each year on February 6, day of the Waitangi Treaty. According to the Maori translation of that treaty, they are a sovereign nation. They have a monarch who lives at Turangawaewae Marae, near the city of Hamilton. Normally the *marae* is closed to outsiders, but during March it is open for the Ngaruawahia Regatta. During the regatta many Maori canoes, called *waka*, compete on the Waikato River.

80 million years ago, when today's continents were all part of a super-continent called Godwanaland, a piece called Zealandia broke loose and drifted out to sea. 60 million years ago it became wedged between two giant tectonic plates. At this boundary the Pacific Plate is pushed beneath the Indo-Australian Plate into Earth's hot interior, fueling active volcanoes. Zealandia became separated into a North Island and South Island, the place Tasman called New Zealand.

The Taupo Volcanic Zone stretches from Tongariro National Park to White Island. From the snow-covered peak of **Mount Ruapehu**, tallest on North Island, eight giant glaciers flow. Mount Ngauruhoe saw movie fame when it played "Mount Doom" in *Lord of the Rings* movies. (The Hobbiton set may be seen in North Island.)

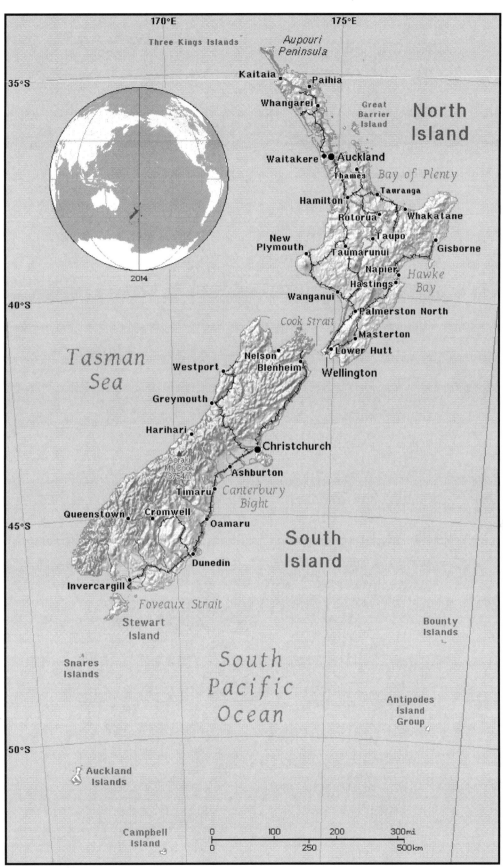

NEW ZEALAND

The volcanic plateau of Rotorua was called "Hades" by George Bernard Shaw, but has many hot attractions. **Lake Taupo** marks the site of an immense eruption, largest of Earth's last 70,000 years.[lxxii] The Maori rock carvings on Lake Taupo's shore are worth the trip. Nearby we can see geysers, bubbling mud pools, Steaming Cliffs, and Earth's biggest boiling lake.

I could recognise the rotten egg smell of **Sulfur Springs**, the same odor found near Kilauea Crater. I found that hiking Hawaii's Big Island is good preparation for the Taupo Volcanic Zone.

White Island in the Bay of Plenty is the Zone's most active volcano. On December 9, 2019 the volcano erupted taking the lives of over a dozen visitors. The landscape of the island is often compared to the Moon or Mars. White Island marks the northern end of a volcanic fault line. 50 miles farther into the sea, the submerged Whakatane Volcano erupts and will someday form another island. White Island marks the start of the Pacific Rim of Fire, where islands are born.

The Maori remember a very ancient homeland, a place where the Sun rises. In this land trees are without leaves for six months of the year. Men can walk on water, as they do when it turns to ice. Maori memories of their origin are a good description of Alaska and the Pacific Northwest.

The Maori tell tales of the demigod Maui, who came from Hawai'i, fishing islands from the sea. The North Island is known as Te-Ika-a-Maui or Maui's fish. Maui is said to have travelled east, to the land of gods and ancestors, to obtain *kumara* the sweet potato.[lxxiii] Maui's canoe *Nukutaimemeha* is said to still be on Mount Hikurangi on North Island. We visited Maui's home in Hawaii, where Maori still travel to South Point to honour their ancestors.

Maori and Hawaiians share those ancestors. Hema, a man born in Hawaii seven generations after Maui-akalana or about 830 AD, also appears in Maori genealogy. Hema's son Kahai, grandson Wahioloa and great grandson Laka appear in that order among Hawaiians and Maori. Multiple generations in a row with the same names show that these ancestors were the same men.

North Island

Kupe the Navigator, who also sailed from Hawai'i, is aid to have landed at North Island about 950 AD. The Maori tell many stories of Kupe, who is as revered as Captain Cook is by Europeans.

Kupe is thought to have landed at Te-au-kanapanapa (Flashing current), a point to the east of Whangaroa Harbour. A monument to Kupe is at Taipa in Doubtless Bay, another place he landed. He brought his wife, Hine, who named *Aotearoa*, "Land of the long white cloud". Kupe also brought a dog named Tauaru, his companion during landings as Stickeen would be for John Muir. At Porirua Harbour he left an anchor stone from the hill Maunga Roa (named after Mauna Loa on Hawaii), on the island of Rarotonga.

Kupe then sailed on to discover South Island. He returned to Hawai'iki from **Hokianga-a-Kupe** (Place of Return), which became one of the main Maori settlements. Kupe's discoveries were passed across many generations. I found many clues that Aotearoa's Maori are descended from Hawaii's *Kanaka Maori.*

The Maori dogs were *kuri*, a breed that has only recently gone extinct. This stuffed specimen is in the Otago Museum in Dunedin, South Island. The *kuri* was barkless. short-haired, short-legged with upright ears. The kuri was very similar to the poi dogs that originated in the Hawaiian Islands.

Olopana, a chief who lived in Hawaii around 1100 AD, sailed south to seek new lands along with his wife Lu'ukia. They appear in Maori history as Koropanga and Rukutia, who sailed from Hawa'iki. Similar names again indicate that Hawaiian and Maori ancestors were the same. Kupe left these voyagers precise directions for reaching Aotearoa from Hawaii.

Whatonga, who was born on an island called Ahu around 1130 AD, grew into a legendary navigator. We have visited Ahu—it is an ancient name for Oahu. An adventurous young man,

Whatonga travelled to Hawa'iki for a big canoe race. During the race, a sudden gale carried the fleet of canoes far out to sea and Whatonga was shipwrecked on the island of Raiatea. His grandfather, a chief named Toi, was grief-stricken. After a long stay at Raiatea, Whatonga rebuilt his canoe and sailed back.

Landing in Hawa'iki, Whatonga found that his grandfather had sailed to find him and disappeared. Whatonga found another canoe, called *Te Hawai* or "From Hawaii". Sailing as far as the island of Rarotonga, he found that Toi had gone toward Aotearoa. Toi's trail led Whatonga to North Island.

Whatonga first landed at Tongaporutu on the West Coast, where he was told that Toi was on the East Coast. He finally found his grandfather living near the Bay of Plenty, at a hilltop fortress called **Kapu-te-rangi.**

The settlement was getting crowded, so Whatonga sailed down the coast and settled at the Mahia Peninsula. His grown sons continued on to find Wellington Harbour. They settled at Somes Island, then later spread to Miramar Island and Kapiti.[lxxiv] Toi and Whatonga left us a detailed history of how Aotearoa was settled.

We can literally follow the trail of these navigators. Above the town of Whakatane is Nga-Tapuwae-o-Toi (the footsteps of Toi). The trail starts near Pohaturoa Rock in the middle of town, then climbs some stairs past a waterfall before ascending to Toi's home of Kapu-te-rangi. If we follow the trail to Ohope Beach, we see many Maori sites and views of the Bay of Plenty.

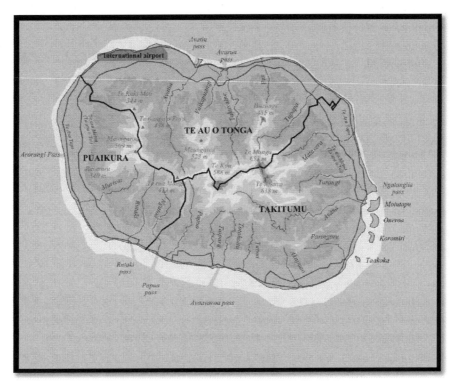

RAROTONGA

Toi's trail stretches back to the Cook Islands and **Rarotonga**. The Royal Road of Toi is the oldest road in the Pacific, dating to the time of Toi. Originally this road, which circles the island, was paved with coral. Today most of Rarotonga's people are Maori, who still often travel to Aotearoa. The names of mountains also travelled from Rarotonga, where one of the tallest is named Arorangi. Many mountains in North Island have been named Aorangi, a name carried by the Maori. (Mauna Kea and Mauna Loa on Hawaii Island are remembered by Maunga Tea and Maunga Roa on Rarotonga.)

By far the largest number of place names in Aotearoa came from Hawaii. Kona on the leeward side of the Big Island (and Haida Gwai'i) is remembered by Tonga Island and Tonga Bay on South Island's leeward side. Kaupo, site of lava flows on Maui, became the Taupo Volcanic Zone. A 2013 study found 518 Aotearoa place names from the Hawaiian Islands, versus only 252 from the Society Islands and fewer from the Tuamoto and Cook Islands.[lxxv]

The DNA of Cook Islanders has mutations at postions 189 and 217, almost exactly like DNA from the Nuu-Chah-Nulth of Vancouver Island. Both peoples also lack a small section of DNA, nine base pairs long, which has somehow been erased. DNA proves that the Maori of the Cook Islands and the Nuu-Chah-Nulth are related.

In Rarotonga we see many dogs running wild. These dogs are short-legged, similar to Hawaiian dogs and the *kuri* of Aotearoa. The Naturalist on one of Captain Cook's voyages noted that the natives called them "poi dogs,"[lxxvi] a nickname that also travelled from Hawaii. Natives of the nearby island of Atiu had never seen dogs, and called the dogs brought by Europeans *Puaka aua*, "Pig that barks".

According to Kupe's directions for Aotearoa, the bows of canoes must point south from two islands called Maui-taha and Maui-pae. These are probably Lanai and Kahoolawe, west of the island of Maui on the Au'au Channel. At Kahoolawe we saw the origin point for voyages south. From there canoes must continue directly south to Rarotonga, where both Whatonga and his grandfather Toi stopped, before turning southwest to reach Aotearoa. Kupe told of losing sight of Hokopa'a, the North Star, and encountering the Southern Cross. This would only happen on a voyage from the Hawaiian Islands, the only Polynesian islands north of the equator. Kupe's directions begin in the Hawaiian Islands.

About 1280 AD more Maori landed in Aotearoa, following the directions Kupe left. We know when these settlers arrived because their footprints are in volcanic ash on the Hauraki Gulf Islands. Another migration occurred around the year 1350 AD, coinciding with the time that Hawaii's first inhabitants were being pushed out of their homeland. Today's Maori still remember the names of the canoes and the chiefs who sailed them.

Paikea, ancestor of tribes on Aotearoa's eastern coast, was said to have sailed from Hawai'iki after another family fight. When he became lost at sea Paikea prayed to the whales for guidance, as Nuu-chah-nulth had done on the other side of the ocean. Answering his prayers, a whale brought Paikea to the shore. Paikea's story is basis of the wonderful film *The Whale Rider*, which ends with the launch of a new Maori canoe. We can visit the beach where it was filmed, Whangara near the town of Gisborne.

In Aotearoa the Maori found gigantic trees, *kauri* and *totara*. Waipoua Forest on North Island is famous for its *kauri*, some of the planet's biggest trees. The largest, called **Tane Mahuta** or "god of the forest," is 1500 years old. Several other trees in the forest are over 1000 years old, dating to the time of Kupe the Navigator. This tree is said to be the offspring of the Sky Father and the Earth Mother. Their story travelled with the Maori from Hawaii to Aotearoa. From these trees the Maori continued the tradition of carving tall ancestor poles.

At Kawhia on the North Island's west coast, one of the original voyaging canoes survives. The canoe called Tai-nui is buried just behind the Makatu meeting house. Stones placed about 75 feet apart mark the canoe's bow and stern. The canoe was moored to a tree at the end of Karewa Street. The tree has multiplied into a clump of trees, a place still remembered by the Maori. The anchor of Tai-nui can be seen at Mokau.

The canoe, the highest achievement of a culture's technology, is another clue to Maori origins. A 2009 study published by Joseph Banks' Royal Society used computers to compare canoe designs from various Pacific island groups. By computing 10 million possible configurations, the study concluded that Maori canoes originated in Hawaii.[lxxvii][lxxviii]

The Nga-rauru tribe, on the west coast of North Island, tells of a sea creature from the place where Maori originated. The **Maraki-hau** has the head of a man, the tail of a fish, and very long distinctive tusks. Such a creature does exist anywhere in the Southern Hemisphere but is easily recognised by Alaskans—the walrus.[lxxix]

The Maori built wooden houses close to the Alaskan design. Carved posts mark their corners and entrances. Figures on the posts represent ancestors—carvings symbolise their bodies. The intricate wall panels, made from native *totara* wood, are as elaborate as those of Saxman or the Chilkat Whale House. Maori houses are not exactly like Alaskan houses, and no two clan houses are identical, for the design has evolved over 2000 years. We can visit many examples of these meeting houses, each one echoing the classic design. The **Tamatekapua Meeting House** in Rotorua is named for the captain of the Arawa canoe.

Mataatua "The House That Came Home" faces the ocean and the Bay of Plenty.

A Maori house from Tokomaru Bay has travelled to Chicago's Field Museum. Illinois Native Americans still use this house for their ceremonies. In their isolation the Maori preserved a culture similar to that of Alaska.

The Waitangi Treaty Grounds near the Bay of Islands contain a Maori meeting house built in 1940, and the giant *Matawhaorua* canoe. When Europeans arrived the Maori rowed to meet them, but sails were occasionally used. Knowledge of sailing crossed the Pacific before Captain Cook. In the nearby Russell Museum we can see a 1/5 scale model of *Endeavour*, which reached the Bay of Islands in 1769.

Nicholas Young was 12 years old, the youngest of *Endeavour's* crew. The ship sailed across seemingly endless ocean searching for a southern continent. On the morning of October 6 Nick climbed the rope ladder to stand his watch in the crow's nest. He caught a glimpse of a point on the horizon that wasn't a cloud, and yelled, "LAND!" This first point would be named for Young Nick.

On October 9 Captain Cook landed at Kaiti Beach, close to today's town of Gisborne and *The Whale Rider* beach. Near the landing site at the foot of Kaiti Hill, a statue of Cook overlooks the Turanganui River. We can also see a statue of Nick Young. When Cook arrived the Maori put up a frightening display, brandishing their weapons and sticking out their tongues. Cook and his crew were treated to the famous Maori *haka* dance, created to frighten strangers!

Endeavour's crew spent 6 months circling the North Island, naming places on the way. The waters near Gisborne seemed starved of supplies, so they were called Poverty Bay. The crew first ventured south past the Mahia Peninsula, where today rockets have been launched into orbit. A place where Maori tried to grab Tupaia's servant became Cape Kidnappers.

Turning north, *Endeavour* found a bounty of food and water, the Bay of Plenty. The Bay has plenty of history, for it was one of the first places Maori settled. I had the privilege of being invited into the Mataatua Meeting House, named for one of the most famous canoes. A Maori woman took me for a walk around the town of Whakatane, pointing out the landmarks used by voyagers to find this Bay.

On November 9 Cook stopped to observe another transit—the planet Mercury crossing the Sun. The nearby town of Whitianga is said to have been founded by Kupe's descendants--the Mercury Bay Museum tells their story. The Polynesian Tupaia found that he could communicate with the Maori, for their languages were related. Another bay was named by the Maori Whangaparaoa or Bay of Whales. Whales were an important part of Maori culture, part of many legends.

Maori still prefer the single canoe, similar to a North American canoe, over the Polynesian outrigger or double canoe. The Maori who met Cook rowed their canoes, though they occasionally used sails. If the Maori are descended from native Alaskans and Hawaiians, then sails may have crossed to Aotearoa.

A lovely natural harbor was named by Cook the Bay of Islands, today home to the Waitangi Treaty Grounds and the *Matawhaorua* canoe. I had the privilege of paddling on another *waka* captained by a Maori chief. We started on the Bay of Islands then went up a river to Haruru Falls. The chief was a walking library of Maori history.

He told me of three Maori homelands: *Hawai'iki-loa* (Long Hawaii, referring to Aotearoa), *Hawai'iki-nui* (Big Hawaii, the Big Island) and *Hawai'iki-pomaumau* (Distant, Haida Gwai'i). Maori canoes striking this coast indicate that they arrived from the Northeast.

Endeavour was not the only European ship in the waters of Aotearoa. French Captain Jean Francois de Surville of the *St Jean Baptiste* was in the sea named for Abel Tasman, sailing clockwise around North Island. At the north tip of North Island, called the tail of Maui's fish by Maori, two paths crossed.

This is **Cape Reinga**, near the northernmost point of Aotearoa. Kupe the Navigator named this place Rerenga Wai-rua, jumping point for spirits on the way back to Hawai'iki. Here waters of the Pacific and Tasman Seas meet--Maori called them the male and female seas. *Wai* means water and *rua* means two, indicating that the soul is composed of two entities. On Kauai we have seen the Wailua River, which also means "two waters".

In a storm on the night of December 16 both *Endeavour* and *St. Jean Baptiste* rounded Cape Reinga, passing within 25 miles, without seeing each other! De Surville did not see that his crew ate their vegetables, and was rapidly losing them to scurvy. In desperation he crossed the Pacific all the way to Peru, where he drowned while trying to go ashore and his crew became Spanish prisoners.

Circling North Island, *Endeavour* anchored at an inlet near Tasman's Murderers Bay. Climbing a hill, Cook saw the inlet turn into a passage to the open Pacific. *Endeavour* sailed through the passage, which would be called Cook Strait. After circling North Island, the ship steered into the unknown South.

South Island

South Island is called "Maui's canoe" by the Maori. I have searched the Pacific for a place that mirrors Alaska. I was pleased to discover, as the Maori ancestors may have, that South Island is a place of mountains and glaciers. Mount Cook at 12,316 feet is the tallest--Maori call it **Aoroki** or Cloud Piercer.

In legend the mountain was formed after a boy named Aoroki came from the skies to visit Papa, the Earth Mother. Hawaiian stories of the Earth Mother have also reached South Island.

Rivers of ice and water flow from South Island's mountains. **Tasman Glacier**, flowing below Aoroki, is the greatest ice river of the southern hemisphere. From Terminal Lake at the foot of the glacier we can see ice calving into the water.

Fox and **Franz Joseph glaciers** descend from the Southern Alps almost to sea level, and are excellent places to hike. If Ketchikan in Alaska is Salmon Capitol of the World, then Rakaia is Salmon Capitol of South Island. The rivers near Rakaia are filled with salmon that return to spawn.

As they did in Hawaii, my friends the eagles once flew here. **The Haast Eagle** was one of the largest ever, with a wingspan approaching 10 feet! The eagle's main prey was the giant flightless *Moa* bird. The *Moa* grew to over 500 pounds, an irresistible meal. They grazed on native grasses, doing the same job as cows in a place without land mammals. Easy prey, the *Moa* was hunted to extinction by humans, causing the eagles to also disappear. The existence of eagles is fragile--even in America they were endangered with extinction.

The Kaikoura Coast is famed for its deep waters full of sea life. A mixture of warm and cold Pacific currents brings nutrients to the surface to feed the fish. We can see fur seals gather at Ohau Point, North of Kaikoura. The seafood buffet also draws Orcas and their cousins the dolphins, keeping sea mammals here year-round. Whale Watch, a business owned by the Ngati Kuri people, runs tours. From a boat we can see pods of **sperm whales**. They were once the most common whales in Hawaii, but hunting drove them to Aotearoa like the Maori. The Maori call Kohola the whale *Tohora*. Unlike the humpbacks, which feed on tiny plankton, toothed sperm whales battle the Giant Squid.

   The Sperm Whale's head contains a giant reservoir of fine-grade oil. While the whales were once hunted for their oil, the purpose of whale oil has long been a mystery. As I listened to the whales, they told me its purpose. The oil reservoir increases the aperture of their sonar signal, improving its *Resolution*. This is the same principle by which telescopes with larger mirrors have better vision. I have also listened to the secret world of nuclear submarines. A submarine's bow also conceals a spherical oil reservoir as an aid to sonar. Whale oil allows the hunt for Giant Squid in the inky dark.

The Giant Squid is one of the most mysterious and feared of sea creatures. It is in sailor's nightmares as the *Kraken*, which could grab small ships and drag them to the bottom. The Giant Squid grows as long as the Hubble Space Telescope, over 55 feet! The eight main tentacles and two longer grasping tentacles are studded with powerful suckers. The huge eyes, big as beachballs, are the largest of any creature on the planet. Like a telescope, a wide aperture allows the squid to see in the dark. The Giant Squid and its cousin the Colossal Squid lurk in the deep waters surrounding South Island, only rarely seen by human eyes.

Kupe the Navigator is said to have explored South Island to battle a giant *wheke*, which is translated to "octopus" but may have been a Giant Squid. The Maori vocabulary does not distinguish between them. (When battling the tentacles of a giant creature, we have difficulty telling whether it's an octopus or a squid!) The story of a huge *wheke* has truth in Aotearoa's Giant Squid.

Stewart Island sits near the tip of South Island. In legends Stewart Island was the anchor of Maui's canoe when he pulled the other islands from the sea. Oban, the only town on the island, contains the Rakiura Museum with exhibits on the Maori settlers. At Big Glory Bay we can see colonies of seals and a salmon farm. Dipping into the Pacific currents, Stewart Island was once a port for whalers and seal hunters.

Stewart Island is the place to go "Kiwi Spotting". Boats take us to Little Glory Bay, where we hike through the bush to Ocean Beach. At sunset we can witness the Stewart Island Brown Kiwi feeding. Kiwi live in pairs and mate for life, another threatened national symbol. The neighbouring Muttonbird Islands and Titi Islands are breeding ground of the Sooty Shearwater, another bird that migrates from Alaska. From October to April we can see them land. During April the local Maori still harvest the Sooty Shearwater for food. Birds were clues for Alaskan voyagers.

One bird alien to Maori was the chicken! Maori starting with Kupe the Navigator kept dogs, but not chickens until Captain Cook brought them. Even a nearly flightless bird is a clue to early navigation. Alaskans and the earliest Hawaiians knew dogs, but not *Pua'a* the pig or the chicken.

The later farm animals arrived in Hawaii from the region of Fiji after 1000 AD.[lxxx] The natives of Fiji and Samoa, even on the fictional island of Disney's *Moana,* did not keep dogs. Dogs and their humans left a trail to Aotearoa from Hawaii and Alaska.

Endeavour's crew orbited south past Stewart Island. On the way Captain Cook charted the coast, producing incredibly accurate maps. By making astronomical observations of the Moon, he was able for the first time to establish the islands' longitude. On March 13 the ship rounded the tip of South Island, proving it was not part of a continent. Slightly disappointed, the crew anchored again in the Cook Strait, on the far side of the world from England. They could return either east or west. Cook and his crew decided on west, and headed into danger.

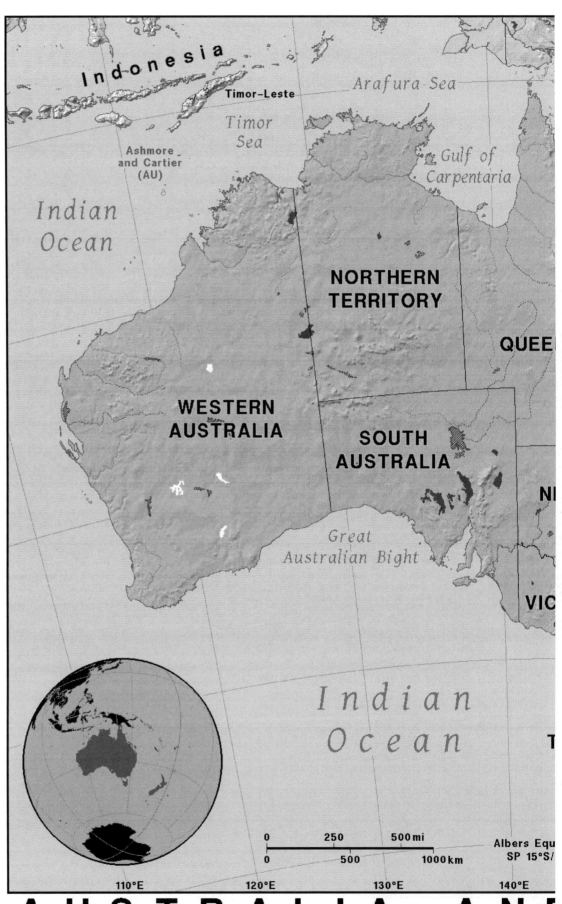

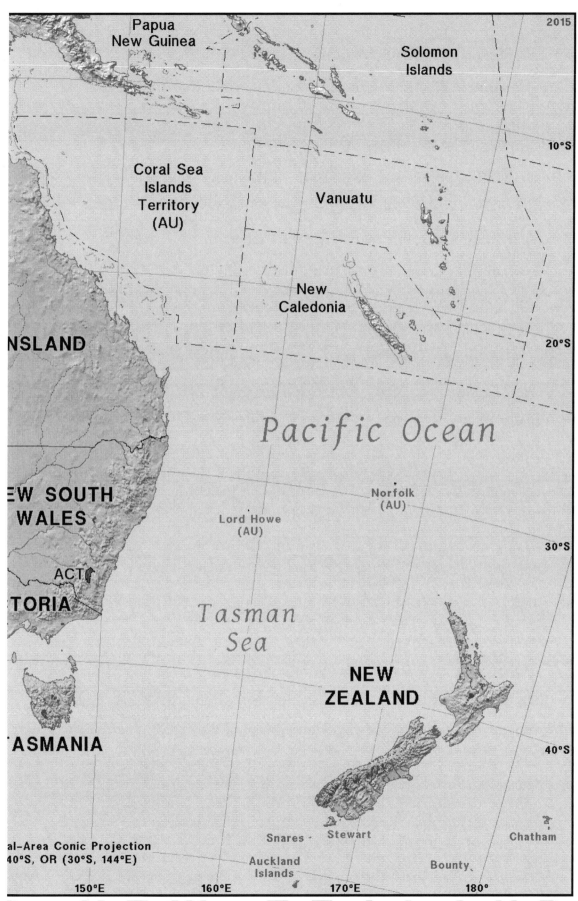

Australia

The continent of Australia was once part of a super-continent called Godwanaland, but broke free millions of years ago. In its isolation the young continent developed many unique life forms. Marsupials from the kangaroo to the Tasmanian Devil fill roles that mammals fill elsewhere. In Tasmania I saw the famous Devils, which are threatened by a mysterious disease. I would like to have seen the Tasmanian Tiger, not a mammal but another marsupial, but they are thought to have gone extinct a century ago. The only land mammals found in Australia are introduced, like the species that builds boats.

In isolation Australia developed a unique culture. Australia's aborigines are not Polynesians, but migrated from across the ocean in the distant past. No one knows how long aborigines have been here. Most estimates say at least 50,000 years, long after Australia had separated from Godwanaland. The only way to reach Australia was by crossing the sea. By their presence the aborigines show that early humans, even tens of thousands of years ago, traveled the ocean.

Captain Cook and his crew intended to reach Tasmania, but Pacific winds blew them many miles off course. As the sun rose on the morning of April 19 land was sighted. It was Australia's east coast, which no European had seen before. On April 29 they found a bay to anchor in. Aborigines with spears appeared on the shore, but ran away. Joseph Banks enjoyed the chance to collect new specimens. Cook named the landing site Botany Bay, then sailed north into a trap.

The Great Barrier Reef is the largest coral structure and some of the best diving on the planet. It is a seemingly endless universe to explore, thousands of miles of reef shared by a billion colourful creatures. This city beneath the sea is the most complex of ocean ecosystems. Today divers enjoy the Barrier Reef, but it was a trap for unwary ships. Captain Louis De Bougainville steered away from the Barrier Reef to avoid being grounded. Captain Cook and *Endeavour* nearly sank in it.

Sailing North along the coast, *Endeavour's* crew started seeing coral reefs with waves breaking over them. The Barrier Reef opens like a funnel in the South and then narrows to trap a ship. Cook and his crew became surrounded by a maze of coral. On the night of June 10 they suddenly heard a grinding noise--*Endeavour* had struck the Reef.

Everything available was thrown overboard to lighten the ship, but they were stuck on the Reef at high tide. The ship began taking on water, so every available man worked the pumps to keep from sinking. As night fell, all hands went to the capstan to try dragging the ship off with the anchor. As shirtless sailors groaned and pushed, the ship budged and then slowly slid free.

Still taking on water, *Endeavour* bobbed toward the shore. The ship ran aground at the mouth of a small river. The crew would be thankful for *Endeavour's* flat bottom--an ordinary ship would not have survived. The crew would recover for two months at a place they named Endeavour River. Today we can see an anchor and cannon jettisoned by *Endeavour* at the James Cook Museum in Cooktown.

Marooned in Australia, the crew found a strange new world. Joseph Banks had plenty of time to collect specimens. For the first time Europeans saw a kangaroo. The aborigines observed these strange people, but kept their distance for days before approaching. Tupaia could not understand the Maori--the language of Australia was completely alien.

After many repairs, *Endeavour* finally sailed out of her river. The ship was still surrounded by reefs, then a passage into open sea appeared. Cook found and sailed through the strait between Australia and New Guinea, discovered by Spanish Captain Luis

Torres in 1606 AD but not seen since. Passing the southern shore of New Guinea, they reached Abel Tasman's port of Batavia on October 10.

The Dutch port was not a place of safety, for it was dirty and full of disease. Cook's attention to his men's nutrition had resulted in not a single loss to scurvy, but Batavia took its toll. In the next few weeks 30 of them would die from malaria and other diseases. Tupaia their guide caught an illness and joined the sailors lost at sea. He would not be the last Polynesian to fall from European illnesses. On the voyage home a mourning bell tolled many times.

On July 10, 1771 Nick Young again sighted land, the coast of England. After anchoring, Cook left the ship carrying an armful of charts and reports. He caught a coach into the streets of crowded London. The officers at the Admiralty were happy to see Cook alive, having circled the world for the Royal Navy. Returning to Mile End Road, James Cook was reunited with Elizabeth after 3 years.

Cook's first voyage did not result in fame-- Joseph Banks became the hero. James Cook was promoted to Commander, and enjoyed an audience with King George III. The King enjoyed the distraction from his troubles with the American colonies. James and a pregnant Elizabeth took a coach to Yorkshire to visit Cook's father, who had never been as far as London. The roads were rough in winter, and Elizabeth felt ill when they reached the stone cottage. Leaving Elizabeth with his father and borrowing a horse, Cook rode alone to the sea.

In Whitby he visited the house where he lived as an apprentice. In 1772 Elizabeth had a son, named for the King, but little George did not survive a year. The voyaging goat, who had sailed around the world twice on different ships, peacefully passed away on the Cook family's property. Cook already planned a return to the Pacific. The Admiralty realised the importance of Cook's discoveries, and gave him two new ships.

Resolution and Adventure

Cook's second voyage would take him past "The Roaring Forties" and the Antarctic Circle. Recently we have found another river, called the Tasman Flow. It flows from Cape Horn eastward through the South Atlantic, Indian and Pacific Oceans, nearly circling the world. The high winds and currents of the southern latitudes are a constant danger. Cook planned to use Aotearoa as a base for fresh water and supplies. Today it is often a staging point for trips to the South Pole.

Endeavour had seen her most adventurous days, and returned to a life carrying cargo. She would be used for carrying troops to America, and is thought to have been sunk in Newport Harbour in 1778. For safety two ships would set out on the voyage, *Resolution* and *Adventure*. Cook's near-disaster on the Barrier Reef had taught him to bring an extra ship.

Joseph Banks, newly famous, wished to command the expedition himself. Banks insisted that *Resolution* be built taller to accommodate a larger entourage. An extra deck and a round deckhouse was built, so tall that the ship could barely stay upright in the Thames. After the Admiralty ordered the Banks house removed, he angrily left the voyage.

For finding longitude, *Resolution* carried a new Harrison Chronometer. If the Sun or another star was seen passing overhead exactly 12 hours before it passed over Greenwich, the observer was 180 degrees from England. Each hour corresponds to 15 degrees. Measuring the time at sea was the difficult part. Britain set up a Board of Longitude with a prize for whoever solved the problem. John Henry Harrison, a self-taught clockmaker, spent a lifetime trying to win the prize. Harrison's chronometer proved to be an accurate way of measuring longitude.

Maori tell the story of Ui-te-Rangiora, who around 650 AD sailed a fleet of canoes south past the island of Rapa Nui. He is said to have seen "rocks that grow out of the sea in the space beyond Rapa"[lxxxi] which could be a description of icebergs. On remote Enderby Island at 51.5 degrees south, less than 1000 nautical miles from the Antarctic Circle, remains of settlements have been found with bones of humans and dogs dating to 1350 AD. The Maori settlers on Enderby Island would have seen icebergs, which can survive at 40 degrees south. In 1721 Dutch Captain Jacob Roggeveen sailed around Cape Horn and also saw floating ice. Since seawater was not known to freeze on its own, Roggeveen thought that the ice calved from the glaciers of an unknown southern land. On Easter Sunday of 1721 Roggeveen found Rapa Nui and named it Easter Island. Polynesians may have explored South 1000 years earlier.

On July 13, 1772 *Resolution* and *Adventure* sailed from Plymouth. They continued into the South Atlantic until they saw icebergs that looked like mountains. The crews observed that the ice appeared blue. On December 14 they encountered a wall of packed ice. Fog descended on the ships; when the fog cleared the sails were full of icicles. They reached latitudes that no ship from Plymouth had sailed before.

On January 17, 1773 Cook's crew became first to cross the Antarctic Circle, 67.5 degrees South. That day they saw giant icebergs lined up in their path. Not wishing to become trapped, Cook ordered the ships to turn north. Today we know that they were only 75 miles from the Antarctic continent. On February 8 in thick fog *Adventure* disappeared. After searching among the ice for days, *Resolution's* crew headed for Aotearoa in case the other ship made it there. Centuries earlier Toi and his grandson Whatonga had both sailed to Aotearoa in hope of meeting. On May 11 Cook found *Adventure* in Queen Charlotte Sound. The two ships left on June 7, searching for a continent until ice forced them back.

On August 16 *Resolution* and *Adventure* were in sight of Tahiti, but the winds died and the ships drifted toward the reefs. Unlike canoes, Cook's ships could not easily be rowed out of danger. Waves pounded *Resolution's* hull against the coral. Finally his ships escaped to anchor again in Matavai Bay. The stress made Cook noticeably ill, so tired that he could barely reach his bunk. Encounters with ice and reefs would push Cook's health to its limits.

The ships lingered 2 weeks in Tahiti while Cook and the crew recovered. The naturalists found their first specimen of the Pacific Golden Plover. Tahitians told Cook that the Plover did not nest there, but migrated from the North. The little birds were a clue that unknown islands lay northward.

Sailing from Tahiti on September 1, two ships explored the Tonga Islands and headed for Aotearoa. In a gale *Adventure* was lost again. *Resolution* reached Queen Charlotte Sound, but this time the other ship was not there. Cook left a message in a bottle for other ships to find, then *Resolution* continued alone. As *Resolution* reached 71 degrees south, the ship encountered a seemingly endless wall of ice. Cook, again feeling ill, reluctantly ordered a turn about.

As the ship turned Midshipman George Vancouver, 14 years old, climbed out to the end of the bowsprit. He waved his midshipman's hat and screamed *Ne Plus Ultra!* (None farther!) For the rest of his life Vancouver would claim to have been closer to the South Pole than anyone. Antarctica would be left for another *Discovery*.

As *Resolution* sailed north Captain Cook's digestive system broke down. The constant stress of navigating the ocean took its toll. Cook could not hold down food or rise from his bunk. The crew thought that the end was near. Finally a bowl of hot soup revived him. While Cook was recovering the Easter Island Rapa Nui appeared before him. Though Cook could barely stand, he and his crew marveled at the mysterious stone heads. After Cook's illness, he sailed for Tahiti expecting to find peace.

At Matavai Bay on April 22, 1774, Cook found a Tahitian fleet preparing for war. The sound of war drums filled Matavai Bay. 300 canoes filled with warriors were preparing to invade a neighbouring island. One war canoe measured 109 feet, long as *Resolution*. Leaving Tahiti and one war, Cook discovered New Caledonia and made yet another stop in Aotearoa. *Resolution* explored Cape Horn and the South Atlantic on the long way home.

Returning to England on July 30 of the next year, Cook found a British fleet preparing for war. It was 1775 and Britain's colonies on the island of America were in rebellion. Lost *Adventure* had safely returned to England the year before. On the way *Adventure* picked up a Polynesian named Omai, who had become a hit in London society. Repairs to

Resolution were rushed because other ships were in line. The wooden ship would suffer many problems on its next voyage.

Though his ships played no part in that war, Cook became a hero. He was promoted to full Captain and made a fellow of the exclusive Royal Society. He had an audience with King George III, who enjoyed a distraction from the war. Captain Cook was given a safe posting at the Greenwich Naval Hospital, where he could have easily finished his career. At Greenwich's Maritime Museum, I and others have enjoyed the mementoes of his life.

Safely home, Cook did not find peace. There was still an ocean to explore and wonders to be found. He still had an ambition to go not only farther than man had been, but as far as it was possible to go. Despite his near-death on the second voyage, Cook became impatient with life on land. The Admiralty recruited Cook for one last mission, to Alaska. *Resolution and Discovery*

Cook's final, fatal voyage is most important in this story. His crew would be the first Europeans to encounter natives of Hawaii and Vancouver Island. Cook would again command the hastily repaired *Resolution*. Captain Charles Clerke commanded a newly commissioned ship, *Discovery*. Midshipman George Vancouver continued as part of the crew-we will see again the names of Vancouver and *Discovery*. Publicly the mission was to bring home Omai, who had been brought to England on *Adventure*.

As on his first voyage, Cook also had a secret mission. He was to search for a Northwest Passage from the Pacific to the Atlantic. The coastline of Alaska and the Pacific Northwest was still in a fog of mystery. Access to America's west coast was desired by France, Spain and Russia. A shortcut to the Pacific was a holy grail for explorers.

Spanish galleons had been crossing the Pacific since the 16th century. They learned that the best way east was to sail into northern latitudes and take advantage of the Kuroshio Current. Though this route missed Hawaii, Juan Gaetano in the 1540's reported several islands which he named La Mesa, Los Monges, and La Desgraciada. Gaetano placed these mysterious islands a thousand miles to the west of Hawaii, for he did not have a good way of finding longitude. The identity of these islands is still a mystery.

Resolution and *Discovery* left England on July 12, 1776. Unknown to the crew, the American colonies had declared independence the week before. The ships stopped in Cape Town for repairs, because *Resolution* leaked badly. On February 12, 1777 Cook anchored in Aotearoa for the last time. The Maori were afraid that he might take revenge for the past, but Cook brought no ill will. He safely delivered Omai to the island of Huahine, home of temples and chiefs.

Cook lingered four months in the islands of Tahiti. He suffered pain from rheumatism, so a Tahitian chief sent 12 girls to massage the pain out. Before leaving in December 1777, Cook asked the Tahitians if they knew any islands to the North. They knew of none, for those voyages had ended centuries before. The two ships headed into seemingly empty ocean.

In his voyages Cook gained the skill of Pacific navigators, to pull islands from the sea. While *Resolution* and her crew were in the middle of the Pacific, Cook alone sensed the presence of land. Cook set lookouts, and on January 18, 1778 they beheld the cliffs of Kauai. Forgotten by Polynesians, our Hawaiian Islands were discovered again by Captain Cook.

Cook went ashore near the Waimea River. The natives prostrated themselves before him, as of he were a visiting god. After Kauai the ships stopped in Niihau for more provisions. Cook wrote that discovery of Hawaii was "the most important that had been hitherto made by Europeans throughout the extent of the Pacific Ocean". He wished to linger in our Islands, but left Niihau on February 2.

On March 7 the lookouts sighted the Oregon coast, a place they called Cape Foulweather. Sailing north, they found respite from the winds at Yuquot, the port they named Friendly Cove. The Nuu-chah-nulth welcomed the voyagers from distant England. Cook noted that the *adze* was exactly alike from the Northwest to New Zealand. Cook also saw women making cloth from bark, exactly as was done by the Maori.

He thought that the blankets of Nuu-chat-nulth looked exactly the same. Even the club he was given as a gift looked exactly like a Polynesian or Maori club. At Friendly Cove Cook may have found the place where voyagers sailed to Hawaii.

As his ships continued Northwest, Cook was again bedeviled by foul seas. He saw and named Mount Fairweather but didn't find Glacier Bay because it was blocked by fog and ice. They sailed into a place they thought were a river, though today we know it as Cook Inlet. The place they turned back was named Turnagain Arm. Near Alaska they again sighted a Golden Plover. Cook wondered if their nest lay even farther North.

The quest took Captain Cook through the Aleutian Islands, where the first Americans had voyaged thousands of years before. Cook encountered the stormy seas of Ha'aleiwawahilani, the Arctic Ocean that Mr. Alaska and Woman of Dreams may have seen. The artists sketched creatures they had never seen before, including polar bears. The crew confronted the walrus, the creature remembered by the Maori as the Maraki-hau. As the ocean filled with ice, they passed through the Bering Strait and the Arctic Circle. At 71 degrees, as far North as they had reached South on the previous voyage, another wall of ice blocked their path. Captain Cook could sail no farther.

Though he had planned to spend Winter in the Kamchatka Peninsula, Cook decided to return to Hawaii. As his ships anchored near Maui, they were visited by Kamehameha the future King. The two ships anchored within a half mile of Waipio Valley, then sailed around the Big Island's windward side of in search of an anchorage. On January 17 a boat commanded by Lieutenant William Bligh reported finding a safe harbour. Captain Cook's last stop was at Kealakekua Bay.

Tens of thousands of people appeared on the shore of the bay. Cook's crew saw the biggest fleet they had ever seen, over 800 canoes! The Big Island was at the time a gathering place and the most populous of the islands. Cook's crew estimated the population at 400,000 but some today say it was closer to one million. Our island supported several times more people than today, possibly as many as lived in London! On January 25 King Kalani'opu'u of the Big Island arrived in a huge canoe.

When Captain Cook went ashore the natives prostrated themselves and greeted him with the chant, "LONO". Unknown to Cook, his arrival coincided with a prophecy, the return of the god called Lono. The *Makahiki* season, which celebrates Lono, runs from October to late January. Arriving at the climax of this festival, Cook was treated as a god. Hawaiians gave him very bit of food and supplies he wished for. Despite the warm welcome, Cook sailed February 4.

The day after leaving Kealakekua Bay, Cook's ships were caught in a sudden storm, just as Whatonga had been caught centuries before. *Resolution's* foremast, which had been poorly repaired in England, snapped. Seeing the ship return with a broken mast, the Hawaiians who had thought Cook a god were not as welcoming. Cook anchored for the last time in Kealakekua Bay and hurried to repair the mast. He sent men ashore in *Resolution's* cutter, largest of their ship's boats. The Hawaiians became bold about theft, causing iron nails to disappear.

On the morning of February 14, 1779 the ship's cutter was gone from its mooring, stolen from beneath *Resolution's* shadow. Cook lost his temper, and stormed ashore in another boat to recover it. In the village he found King Kalani'opu'u, who agreed to go aboard *Resolution* as a bargaining chip. As they reached the shore of Kealakekua Bay, an angry crowd gathered around them. A line of *Resolution's* Marines tried to guard their boats. Cook and his landing party were outnumbered. A cry ran out, then gunshots, and the shore descended into melee. Cook turned to yell something to his men, but was struck from behind. As he fell, the crowd of natives descended upon him. On the shore of Kealakekua Bay, Captain Cook's blood was spilled.

Both British and Hawaiians realised that a terrible tragedy had occurred. Four Royal Marines also fell in the fray. Giving Cook the treatment given to the greatest chiefs, the regretful Hawaiians returned what was left of his remains. Lieutenant Clerke, who took command of the voyage, chose not to seek revenge. Under Clerke's command, they returned to Alaska to continue the mission. Lieutenant Clerke would fall to illness before they voyage was over. The mysterious origin of Hawaiian and Polynesian voyagers remained unsolved.

In his final voyage Cook may have found not just Hawaii but the *Wao Lani* the first Hawaiians sailed from. He even encountered the *Maraki-hau,* the walrus from the land where Maori originated. By the early 19th century many scholars thought that Polynesian voyagers originated in North America. If Captain Cook had lived, his authority could have added to these voices. The origin of Hawaiians might have been settled two centuries ago.

In the wake of European voyages, the population of Hawaii fell victim to disease. Venereal disease, smallpox and measles all took a toll. Population of the Big Island, which once supported as many people as London, would fall to a fraction of that. Peoples of Alaska, the Pacific Northwest, and islands like Tahiti all suffered. Long-distance voyages to Hawaii were largely forgotten.

Astrolabe and Boussole

Comte de La Perouse, an aristocrat, soldier and a scholar, was chosen by **King Louis XVI** to explore the Pacific after Cook. La Perouse enjoyed visiting the Paris Observatory, where Ole Roemer had first measured THE SPEED OF LIGHT. He named his first ship *Astrolabe* after the navigator's instrument. In August 1785 La Perouse sailed in *Astrolabe* along with a second ship *Boussole* and an entourage of artists and naturalists. He hoped to chart areas of the Northwest that Cook had missed. La Perouse became the first European to visit the island of Maui and remote Mokumanamana or Necker Island. After Hawaii, the two ships sighted the Alaskan coast on June 23.

La Perouse stopped to explore Lituya Bay, within today's Glacier Bay National Park. The Tlingit warned La Perouse that the waters were treacherous. Lituya Bay is shaped like a letter T, exiting into the Pacific through a narrow strait. La Perouse sent the crew of a boat to take soundings, but a huge tide rushed through the strait and drowned all 21 men. Lituya Bay showed that the Northwest coast could be dangerous.

After 2 ½ years of exploring, La Perouse's ships reached Australia and the British settlement at Botany Bay. There he left all his notes and charts to be forwarded to France. Possibly La Perouse anticipated that he, like Cook, might not return home. In February 1788 La Perouse's ships sailed into the Pacific for the last time and disappeared. At home, his King Louis XVI fell to the French Revolution and the guillotine. In the 1960's researchers found wreckage of the French ships in the Solomon Islands. In 2016 an anthropologist uncovered a fantastic story: La Perouse's crew built another ship, reached Australia, and were shipwrecked again on the Barrier Reef! Had the aristocrat La Perouse returned to France, he would have fallen to the Revolution.[lxxxii]

Discovery and Chatham

Two weeks after returning from the third voyage, **George Vancouver** passed his exams for lieutenant. He grew up to command his own voyage of exploration. He inherited the mission to chart the Pacific Northwest coast in search of a Northwest Passage. Vancouver named his ship *Discovery*-- not the same ship from Cook's third voyage, but a new ship named in Cook's honour.

KARAKAKOA BAY, OWYHEE, DRAWN BY THOMAS HEDDINGTON, ARTIST WITH VANCOUVER.

Discovery and Chatham sailed from Plymouth on April 1, 1791. Stopping in Hawaii, Vancouver was determined to have good relations with the natives. After Cook's death Hawii's royal court moved to the safety of Waipio valley, where Kamehameha had influence. Vancouver brought Hawaiians the first horses they had ever seen. Today horses wander freely in Waipio Valley, the only wild herd in Hawaii. Kamehameha also admired *Discovery's* cannons, but Vancouver diplomatically said that the guns were property of King George III and could not be sold. Kamehameha was impressed by stories of this distant king, his empire, and his ships full of trained men like Vancouver. He was inspired to become King of all the Hawaiian Islands.

Ships of Vancouver and Spaniards at Friendly Cove, Nootka, 1792.

On April 16, 1792, one year after leaving England the ships arrived at the California coast. Sailing north, the two ships entered the Juan de Fuca Strait into Puget Sound. In search of a Northwest Passage they surveyed the complicated coast and islands of the Northwest. This was painstaking work in small boats, which were on their own for weeks at a time. Often the crews would sleep in their boats because the coast was too dangerous.

In the straits of Juan de Fuca, George Vancouver peacefully met with ships from Spain, who had previously discovered the strait. Boats from *Discovery* and *Chatham* brought the first Europeans into today's Vancouver Harbour. The ships sailed up Johnson Strait, a narrow passage where daily tides turn into a torrent. Even today cruise ships must time their passage through the strait to avoid the tides. The ships circled Vancouver Island and proved that it is an island.

On August 28 Vancouver reached Friendly Cove. British had feared that the Nuu-chah-nulth were cannibals, but a simple test proved them wrong. When Vancouver's crew offered them some venison, the Nuu-chah-nulth were afraid it was human and British were the cannibals! On the way South *Chatham* entered the Columbia River and claimed it for Britain. They passed San Francisco and Monterey Bays before crossing the ocean to Hawaii. As humpback whales learned to do long ago, Vancouver's ships spent Summer in Alaska and Winter in Hawaii.

Captain Vancouver brought the first cattle to Hawaii, 5 California cows and a bull. For native Hawaiians, who had never seen a land animal larger than a pig, a cow was a huge horned monster. It made a terrifying sound never heard in the Islands, *Moooo!* However, after one cow gave birth they eagerly embraced the new calf. Cattle ran wild over the Big Island until King Kamehameha recruited American cowboys to round them up and teach Hawaiians how to manage them. This was the beginning of Hawaii's giant cattle ranches.

On the second Summer in 1793 Vancouver's crew explored the coastline between 52 and 56 degrees north, including Haida Gwai'i. They passed the location of Glacier Bay, but it was completely filled with ice. Only in John Muir's time was Glacier Bay discovered. Again Vancouver chose to explore California on the way to Winter in Hawaii, exploring as far as the Baja Peninsula.

In Summer 1794 the search for a Northwest Passage resumed at Kodiak Island. Returning to waters he had seen in the earlier *Discovery*, Vancouver found that "Cook River" was really Cook Inlet. He found no Northwest Passage, but made detailed charts of the entire coast. He stopped one last time in Friendly Cove before safely returning to England.[lxxxiii]

Vancouver escaped Cook's fate in Hawaii, but in England he was symbolically struck in the back and torn to shreds. A very difficult midshipman named Thomas Pitt claimed that Vancouver had mistreated him. Pitt's uncle was William Pitt the Prime Minister, and their family was powerful. Though he was not convicted of wrongdoing, Vancouver's naval career was finished. Captain Vancouver quietly passed away at the age of 40, ten years younger than his mentor Captain Cook. Today we remember Vancouver for maintaining good relations with Hawaiians while exploring the Pacific. Statues of Vancouver can be seen in King's Lynn, England, Vancouver in Washington State, Vancouver in British Columbia, and atop the Legislative Building in Victoria.

Bounty

William Bligh, a lieutenant on Cook's third voyage, would be remembered as captain of HMS *Bounty*. During 1789 the *Bounty* sailed to Tahiti with a mission of collecting breadfruit trees. Joseph Banks the naturalist had fallen in love with Tahiti's breadfruit, and used his influence in to have the trees exported. Bligh intended to sail around Cape Horn into the Pacific, but weather forced him to detour through the Indian Ocean, passing the southern tip of Aotearoa. Today an anchor from Bounty can be seen at the Maritime Museum in Auckland. In Tahiti, *Bounty* crew members fell victim to the island paradise with its siren song, and didn't want to leave. The mutiny led by Fletcher Christian resulted in Bligh and a few loyal crew being set adrift in the ship's launch.

If anyone doubts whether eight people could voyage to Hawaii in a 40-foot canoe, we remember that Captain Bligh sailed 3,600 miles in 23-foot boat packed with eighteen men. With so many onboard, the boat's freeboard (distance to the water) was the length of one man's hand! Even small waves washed over the boat, so the crew was continually bailing to avoid being swamped. They were short of everything but enemies, having been left with barely 3 days' supplies. The heavy rain was a gift from the skies, for it kept them from dying of thirst. Thanks to Bligh's expert navigation, learned from Captain Cook, the loyal crew reached the Dutch East Indies and safety. Bligh would have welcomed a roomy Haida or Nuu-chah-nulth canoe.

The mutineers led by Fletcher Christian became the first Europeans to stop on the island of Rarotonga, on the way to their self-imposed exile on remote Pitcairn Island. Today many of Pitcairn's inhabitants are descended from Mr. Christian.

Tilikum and Bijaboji

In the 20th century, time of aeroplanes and spacecraft, many people remained fascinated with voyaging the Pacific. In 1901, while the Wright Brothers and Aotearoa's Richard Pearse experimented with aircraft, John Voss acquired a Nuu-chah-nulth canoe nearly a century old. Fitting her with sails, Voss christened the canoe *Tilikum* and sailed into the South Pacific. When his crewmate became ill, Voss continued alone. He sailed to the Cook Islands and eventually reached London.

Voss stopped in Aotearoa to give lectures, traveling to Palmerston at the invitation of a Maori chief. Hundreds of Maori gathered, inspired by the voyage. Voss reinforced the belief that Maori had once crossed the Pacific. One Maori, upon seeing Voss and *Tilikum*, finally believed that his ancestors voyaged in an "Indian canoe".[lxxxiv] Today we can see *Tilikum* in Victoria, British Columbia's Maritime Museum, proof that a Nuu-chah-nulth canoe sailed to Aotearoa.

During 1937 Amelia Earhart tried navigating the Pacific to fly around the world; she and her navigator were never seen again. Almost simultaneously, 22-year old Betty Lowman Carey successfully navigated the Inside Passage from Puget Sound to Ketchikan. She rowed a native Alaskan canoe that had been mysteriously found floating near Puget Sound. Betty was determined to return the canoe to its home in Alaska. Hers was a solo journey of 66 days, across the high seas of Queen Charlotte Sound and Dixon Entrance. Betty lived to retire peacefully in Haida Gwai'i. Her canoe *Bijaboji* still inspires us at the Anacortes History Museum in Washington.[lxxxv]

Kon Tiki

We can't continue without including Thor Heyerdahl of Norway, 20th century voyager. As a Naturalist in the 1930's he did research in the Marquesas Islands. His experience in the Marquesas convinced Heyerdahl that the first Hawaiians did not come from there. During 1939 and 1940 he lived in British Columbia, where he became fascinated by Canada's First Nations. After service in World War 2, during 1947 Heyerdahl embarked on his most famous voyage. *Kon Tiki* was a raft made of South American balsa, the same light wood used in model airplanes. Heyerdahl wished to prove that Polynesian ancestors could have crossed the Pacific.

Heyerdahl was intrigued by the sweet potato, which originated in South America but is grown throughout Polynesia. Maori believe that the demigod Maui brought sweet potatoes from the East. Heyerdahl was also fascinated by the *Tiki* tradition. An Inca hero Con-tici-viracocha was said to have voyaged into the Pacific. Heyerdahl became convinced that the Polynesian *Tiki* was the same hero. His journey was difficult, because Heyerdahl had never sailed before!

On April 28, 1947 *Kon Tiki* was launched from Callao, Peru. Following Pacific currents, the raft drifted 5,000 miles in 102 days before washing ashore in the Tuamoto Islands. The *Kon Tiki* adventure became a bestselling book and an Oscar-winning documentary. It led to a *Tiki* craze in the US, where *Tiki*-styled bars and restaurants became popular coast-to-coast. Thor Heyerdahl's raft can be seen in Oslo's *Kon Tiki* museum, not far from the Norwegian Maritime Museum and the *Fram* Museum.

Heyerdahl also experimented with papyrus boats he christened *Ra* and *Ra II*. His first *Ra* became waterlogged and foundered in the Atlantic. Undaunted, Heyerdahl successfully sailed *Ra II* across the Atlantic to show that ancient Africans could have sailed to America. Voyages of Ancient Africans to the land of the Maya are a subject for another book.

Thor Heyerdahl showed that native Americans could have voyaged the ocean. However, Con-tici-viracocha and *Tiki* probably came from different centuries. DNA from South America is missing the mutation at Position 247, indicating that today's Polynesians probably did not originate there. Though famous for *Kon Tiki*, Heyerdahl was equally interested in another route. From his time in British Columbia, he thought that the first Hawaiians sailed from there. DNA and an ocean of evidence shows that Thor Heyerdahl was on the right course.

Orenda II

During 1978 *Hokulea* and her large crew attempted the passage between Hawaii and Tahiti with tragic results. Shortly after leaving Honolulu she started taking on water and capsized. The canoe's emergency radio floated away. Up to their neck in high seas, the crew was clung to the overturned *Hokulea*. Eddie Akau, a member of the crew and a renowned surfer, paddled his surfboard to get help and was lost. *Hokulea* reminded us of the dangers of voyaging.

Later in 1978 Hawaii was successfully reached from America by a single canoe with a crew of three. Geordie Tocher had a lifelong dream of sailing to Hawaii. His first homebuilt canoe ended as a wreck off California. Filled with *Resolution*, Geordie and his friends carved another 42-foot canoe to a Haida design from a log of Douglas Fir. *Orenda II* carried Geordie and two crewmates 4500 miles from Vancouver to San Francisco and then Hawaii. His crew was greeted by native Hawaiians, native Americans, and even Maori. A chief from Aotearoa told Geordie that Maori had always known that they originated in America. A plaque in Dundareve, West Vancouver, marks the dock where Geordie sailed from. *Orenda II* is preserved nearby, a reminder that Haida canoes crossed the Pacific.

Geordie chose to stop in San Francisco to make the ocean crossing shorter. Captain Vancouver and *Discovery* also visited California on the way to Hawaii. Since canoes from the Northwest often voyaged the coast, Chief Nuu and others may have used this route. The distance to Hawaii from San Francisco's Golden Gate is just 2320 miles, almost exactly the same as from the Marquesas Islands.

The story of Nuu and Hawaii's *Discovery*, which I learned from our High Chief's writings, is remembered by the Maori in much greater detail. Para-whenua-mea lived near the River Tohinga, which flows through the ancient homeland. This land is a *tua whenua,* a continent not an island. It is bordered by high snow-covered mountains, and contains fruited plains where the *kumara* sweet potato grows[lxxxvi]. In this story Para-whenua-mea and his son built a boat before a great flood. His crew included two more men and several women, a crew of eight. The story says they brought along dogs and *kumara,* acknowledging that these came from overseas.

Rising waters took the crew down the River Tohinga, through many cataracts, before reaching a first *Hawai'iki* homeland (Haida Gwai'i). There the crew repaired the boat and saw goddesses dancing on the water (whales, which give birth to live young). For six months they traveled along a shoreline (America's west coast) before venturing into *Moana-nui* (Great Ocean). They drifted for two months before reaching another *Hawai'iki* (The Big Island). Para-whenua-mea and his crew settled on this Hawai'iki, today's Hawaiian Islands.

If anyone doubts that this distance can be rowed, every two years we can watch the Great

Pacific Rowing Race from Monterey, California to Oahu. Crews must travel with the supplies they carry, with no resupply allowed, like early voyagers. Transit to Hawaii typically takes about 60 days, about as long as it took Para-whenua-mea or Nuu.

Marquesas Islanders have a tradition of a homeland called Havai'iki. Their islands were also said to have been fished from the sea by Maui. Hawaiian oral histories tell of Chief Nuu and Hawai'iloa discovering the islands, and of Kana Loa finding the Marquesas. There is no tradition of Marquesans discovering Hawaii, or of Maui fishing Hawaii from the sea. The Marquesas theory appears to be a European infection.

THE SPEED OF LIGHT recounts how humans determined that Earth is spherical. A route from Taiwan region via the Marquesas Islands ignores the globe. The great circle distance from Taiwan to the homeland of Haida Gwai'i is only 5500 miles, with many islands and kelp forests on the way for boat snacks. From Taiwan to the Marquesas is 9800 miles, 40 percent of Earth's circumference, nearly all of it open ocean! *Hokulea* and a fleet of canoes have shown that sailing from the Marquesas to Hawaii is dangerously difficult. Distance and the globe favour the islands of America.

On those islands lived some of history's great navigators. The Haida, Tlingit, Nuu-chah-nulth and other tribes regularly voyaged the Pacific. Contact with Europeans disease ravaged their peoples and a history of voyaging was nearly forgotten. Native American people of various tribes suffered from low esteem. It is vitally important that natives of Alaska and the Northwest remember their heritage.

On the Hawaiian Islands a revival of voyaging has led to a Renaissance in pride, for we are voyagers. From Hawaii, situated near the middle of the Pacific, islands from Haida Gwai'i to Aotearoa are points on a navigator's compass. In canoes built from American logs, early Hawaiians voyaged to Tahiti and other islands in the South. As it has been for many centuries, Hawaii is a centre of Pacific navigation.

An ocean of evidence supports the words of High Chief Solomon Peleioholani. Previously voyaging was thought to have ended in Hawaii, but the adventure stretched to Alaska. This doubles the area that we explored to the entire Pacific. Polynesians are doubly proud of following winds, waves and stars. These currents, along with birds and sea life, favour voyages from North America.

In the later 20th century the Pacific welcomed new explorers. During 1968, the bicentennial of Cook's first voyage, the Apollo 7 mission splashed down in the ocean. The next year *Eagle* landed on the Moon, a momentous event in the history of voyaging. In July 2009, the 40th anniversary, its crewmembers Buzz Aldrin and the late Neil Armstrong visited our group at Johnson Space Center. Moon missions, including another *Endeavour*, splashed down in the Pacific until 1972.

Though I've not yet been into Space, I have been able to follow the trail of great navigators. In following this path, I was reminded that one person can make a difference. I could only imagine the battle between Kupe the Navigator and the tentacles of a giant squid. I could easily identify with the fictional *Moana*, who opposed a great darkness that threatened the ocean. Passing the locations of *Lord of the Rings,* I was reminded of Frodo opposing a great shadow enveloping Middle Earth. In my travels I encountered a greater darkness, in the Universe.

If in the year of 2018 AD you ask most scientists, they tell you that the Universe is dominated by an invisible "dark energy". Scientists say it is repulsive, countering Newton and Einstein's gravity. They say that even now darkness is causing the

Universe to expand at an accelerated rate, and will do so until stars and galaxies are torn from our sight and the planets are ripped apart. This "dark" idea has spread farther than the tentacles of a giant squid. It is considered the most profound problem of science.

By studying nature I found equations that describe the size, shape and origin of the Universe. This act of mind eliminates the need for "dark" energy. Mathematics *predicts* what astronomers have only observed, that the Universe began in a burst of light and is continually expanding. I found that this is not a Universe of "dark" energies, but is filled with light. THE SPEED OF LIGHT tells more about this *Discovery*.

In great admiration of the maps that Cook and navigators drew, I mapped the Universe as a sphere, but in four dimensions rather than three. On this sphere the area that our astronauts have explored is infinitesimally small. At times it may seem a lonely quest, like sailing alone where no one has gone before. This has been an adventure far greater than the distance from Earth to the Moon. Beyond the Pacific is a much greater ocean.

In Hawaii the Milky Way Galaxy is known as I'a, the Fish. In the glowing clouds we can see its giant head and jaws. The movie's *Moana* finds Maui's island by following a starry fishhook in the sky. Fans will be pleased to know that they too can find Maui's fishhook! It is the constellation called Scorpius by Europeans, which looks more like a hook than a scorpion.

Maui was legendary for dragging giant fish from the water with his hook. The curve of Maui's fishhook is lodged in the jaws of I'a. As the fishhook rises in the Southeast, it appears to drag the great fish behind it. In the southern hemisphere the rise of I'a is even steeper and more dramatic. The Maori call the galaxy *Ikaroa*. It is our next destination.

GALAXY

February 24, 2011

    The sky rained on the morning of November 4, so the launch was scrubbed. On a clear day, a million of us came to Cape Canaveral for *Discovery*. She carried the last module for the Space Station. The American tribes could not find the resources to finish the Station alone, so ISS was built with the help of 15 other nations. The contributions of the Russian tribe, which was sometimes a rival but had experience in Space, were critical. After 2011, no craft would launch humans from Cape Canaveral for over eight years....

The crowds gathered at the Causeway viewing area and surrounding beaches for miles around. As the countdown neared Zero, people chanted, "10...9...8..." in unison. There was silence, then flames surrounded the Shuttle. The deafening roar of its engines arrived a moment later, drowning the crowd's cheers. *Discovery* ascended into the air.

At the Cape I proudly watched the launch of **STS-133**, *Discovery's* final flight, having previously been in Florida during 2010 for the earlier attempt. For those of us working at NASA that year, witnessing Shuttle launches was a climax of our dreams and labours. Thousands of people at NASA contributed to shuttle launches. Among Space Shuttles, *Discovery* stands out. She flew into Space 38 times, more than any other Shuttle, traversing 138 million miles. She carried 252 people into orbit. On an earlier flight *Discovery* had made Ellison Onizuka the first Hawaii-born astronaut, before he fell in the *Challenger* accident. On that day in 2011 another Shuttle stood nearby at its own pad, ready in case of an emergency. Spaceflight is risky and expensive--a successful launch is always reason to cheer.

The Pacific Ocean has already played a role in spaceflight. Every Mercury orbital mission, and every Gemini and Apollo mission, splashed down in the Pacific. Like all Shuttles before her, *Discovery* entered Earth's atmosphere over the Pacific, crossing the ocean in minutes. When the Space Station's life is ended, it too will be deorbited into the Pacific. A place is already planned for ISS in the deep waters 3000 miles east of Aotearoa. Plans for space capsules after Shuttle ensure that astronauts will enjoy the warm embrace of the Pacific.

The term "Space Shuttle" originally came from STAR TREK. During the 1960's NASA plans for a winged spacecraft were called an "Integrated Launch and Reentry Vehicle," not a very attractive name. During 1966-1969 STAR TREK introduced the *Shuttlecraft*, a vehicle for travelling between a planetary surface and Space. Many NASA personnel enjoyed watching STAR TREK. In an August 1968 speech before the British Interplanetary Society, George Mueller of NASA mentioned a "space shuttle". This was the first official use of the term. In January 1972 President Richard Nixon formally announced development of a Space Shuttle. The full-scale STAR TREK shuttlecraft, named for *Galileo*, is today on display at Space Center Houston.

We have been briefly introduced to history's biggest story of exploration, 6000 years of voyaging the Pacific. Before anyone thinks the adventure is over, there is greater ocean to explore. The future frontier is I'a, the galaxy. For thousands of years humans have used the stars to navigate Earth and even reach the Moon. Discovering the islands of the Pacific is the model for exploring the galaxy. Within the next 6000 years we can navigate the stars.

Astronauts have one great advantage over ocean navigators—our eyes can see into space. In sea voyages the destination is hidden by Earth's curve. Our naked eye can see the planets and the stars beyond them, even the Andromeda Galaxy. We can see vastness of space, but we need not fear it. Our understanding of space, time and THE SPEED OF LIGHT takes us closer to the stars.

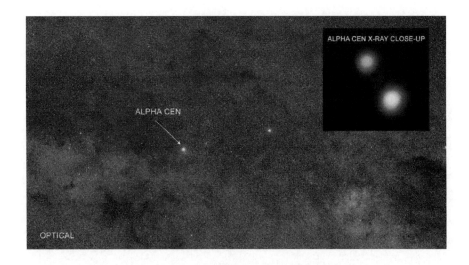

Two pointer stars that help navigators find the South Celestial Pole are Alpha Centauri and Beta Centauri. They are part of a triple system, orbiting one another in a celestial dance. During 2016 astronomers found evidence of a planet with just 1.3 times Earth's mass, orbiting in a habitable zone neither too hot nor cold, around Alpha Centauri.[lxxxvii] These stars have already been reached by writers' imaginations—the fictional moon Pandora of the *Avatar* movies orbits Alpha Centauri.

The third star of this system, Proxima Centauri, is too faint to be seen by the naked eye but is currently the nearest star to our Solar System, just 4.24 light-years away. A ship traveling near the Speed of Light would reach Proxima Centauri in about that many years, comparable to the 4 years Captain Vancouver spent at sea.

Hawai'iloa is said to have followed the seven stars of the **Pleiades** constellation westward to find Hawaii. This cluster about 445 light-years away holds over a thousand stars. In Hawaii the Pleiades are known as Makali'i. When Makali'i rise coincides with the setting Sun it begins the Makahiki season, the Hawaiian New Year that Captain Cook arrived in the midst of. To the Maori the name has become Matariki. When Matariki rises in the Northeast, the Maori New Year begins. Maori call the Pleiades the Eyes of God.

THE SPEED OF LIGHT; 300,000 kilometres or 186,000 miles per second; once seemed an incomprehensible demon. Readers of my previous book know that I've been working to understand and predict light's speed, what it is today and what it was in the past. As I complete this book an atomic clock aboard the International Space Station is being prepared to test that prediction. Our understanding of the Speed of Light is the first step toward reaching it.

We can explore other islands on the way. The goddess Hina, mother of Maui, is said to have left Earth to reside on the Moon. The Moon is a bounty of resources and a training ground for explorers. Our solar system's planets and their many moons are nearby goals, and may even contain life. We may find creatures burrowing into frozen moons, like the Ice Worms of Alaska. Within the watery interiors of moons Europa or Enceladus, we may someday meet with swimming entities like Hawaii's Manta Ray or Aotearoa's Giant Squid. Farther out, a sea of objects in the Kuiper Belt and Oort Cloud extend much of the way to the stars. These distant objects could also contain warmth and life. Like Pacific voyagers on the Kelp Highway, we can find many stops enroute to the stars.

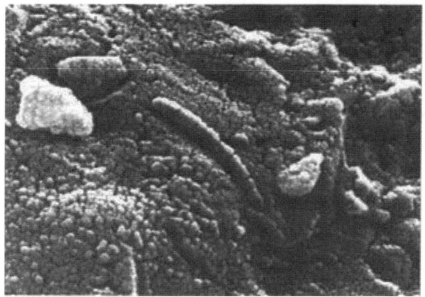

I'a contains over 250 million stars. Reaching the stars of I'a, we have learned, will require infinite patience. Since we have the technology to settle the Moon and and planets, many of us wish we were already doing so. Over the centuries Nuu and other explorers had to wait until their voyages could be mounted. Like their voyages, spaceflight is expensive and potentially dangerous. An unprotected human in space will suffocate like one drowning in the sea. In the Pacific, we have seen clues to the origin of Polynesians and the first Americans.

Among the stars is an even more profound mystery, the origin of life itself. At Johnson Space Center I worked with the scientists who in 1996 found indicators of fossil life on a Martian meteorite 3.5 billion years old. The possible fossils look like tiny versions of Alaska's Ice Worm. If microbial life could have drifted across space to Earth, life may not have originated here. Some research indicates that life began on Mars before traveling to Earth, and that we are all Martians![lxxxviii] This idea was suggested a century ago by the chemist Arrhenius, who believed that life arrived as spores from space.

A study from 2013 used mathematics to measure the increasing complexity of living things. The famous Moore's Law says that computers double in power in a certain number of years. Researchers used a similar law to estimate the complexity of life. Extrapolating toward the past, the study says that life started 10 billion years ago! Our solar system is only 4.6 billion years old, so if life were that ancient it must have started somewhere else.[lxxxix] Someday we could be searching other worlds for the origin of life.

Humans of various faiths believe in a Heaven, a place where gods and ancestors came from. The origin of our life may be in the heavens. As we explore from the Pacific to the ocean of space, we learn more about our beginnings and the origin of the Universe. A heavenly origin is in religions of a God who seeded the universe with life. Our exploration of the heavens brings us closer to the Eyes of God.

LOUISE RIOFRIO
Houston, Texas

References

PROLOGUE: ISLANDS

[i] Riofrio, L., "Space/Time as a possible solution to supernova and other problems," *Proceedings of the 9th Asian-Pacific Regional IAU Meeting* in Bali, Indonesia, 26-29 July 2005 Institut Teknologi Bandung Press, 2006, p.257, http://adsabs.harvard.edu/abs/2006apri.meet..257R

[ii] Shortland, E., *Traditions and Superstitions of the New Zealanders*, London, 1856

[iii] Skinner, Charles M., *Myths and Legends of Our New Possessions and Protectorate,* Philadelphia, J.B. Lippincott, 1900

[iv] Tregear, Edward, *Maori-Polynesian Comparative Dictionary*, Wellington, Lyon and Blair, 1891

[v] Kalakaua, David, and Daggett, Rollin, *The Legends and Myths of Hawaii*, New York, Webster & Co., 1888

[vi] Thorsby, E. et al., "Further evidence of an Amerindian contribution to the Polynesian gene pool on Easter Island," *Tissue Antigens* 73(6) p. 582-5, Jun 2009

[vii] Thorsby, E., "The Polynesian gene pool: an early contribution by Amerindians to Easter Island," *Philos Trans Royal Society London B Biol Sci.* 367(1590) p. 812-9, 19 Mar 2012

[viii] Sykes, B., *DNA USA: a genetic portrait of America*, New York, W.W. Norton, 2012

[ix] Sykes, B., *Seven Daughters of Eve,* New York, W.W. Norton, 2001

[x] Trejaut, J., Lin, M., "Traces of Archaic Mitochondrial Lineages Persist in Austronesian-Speaking Formosan Populations," *PLOS Biology* 3: 8, (2005)

[xi] Fladmark, K. R., "Routes: Alternate Migration Corridors for Early Man in North America," *American Antiquity* 44(1): p. 55-69, 1979

[xii] Pederson et al., "Postglaciation viability and colonization in North America's ice-free corridor," *Nature* 537, p. 45-49, 2016

[xiii] Min-shan Ko, Albert, et al., "Early Austronesians: Into and Out Of Taiwan," *American Journal of Human Genetics* 94: 3, p. 426-435, 2014

[xiv] Erlandson, J.M. Et al., "The Kelp Highway Hypothesis: Marine Ecology, the Coastal Migration Theory, and the Peopling of the Americas," *Journal of Island & Coastal Archaeology*, 2: 2, p. 161–174, 2007

ALASKA: GREAT LAND

[xv] Boeckle, M. and Clayton, N., "A Raven's memories are for the future," *Science* 357: 6347, p. 127-127, 2017

[xvi] *Authentic Hoonah*, Hoonah, 2017

[xvii] Muir, John, "The Discovery of Glacier Bay," *Century*, June 1895

[xviii] Muir, John, *Stickeen: The Story of a Dog*, 1909

[xix] *Marine Mammal Science* 33: 1, p. 1-406, Jan 2017

[xx] Waldman, Carl, *Encyclopedia of Native American Tribes,* New York, Checkmark Books, 1988

[xxi] Greenberg, J.H., *Language in the Americas,* Palo Alto, Stanford University Press, 1987

[xxii] Greenberg, J.H. and Ruhlen, M., "Linguistic Origins of Native Americans," *Scientific American* 267, p. 94-99, 1992

[xxiii] Ward, R.H. et al., "Genetic and linguistic differentiation in the Americas," *Proceedings of National Academy of Sciences* 90, p. 10663-667, 1993

[xxiv] Malhi, R.S. et al., "Patterns of mtDNA Diversity in Northwestern North America," *Human Biology* 76, p. 33-54, 2004

[xxv] Reich, D. et al., "Reconstructing Native American population history," *Nature* 488, p. 370-374, 2012

[xxvi] Campbell, John, "The Origin of the Haidahs of the Queen Charlotte Islands," *Transactions of the Royal Society of Canada* 2, p. 91-117, 1897

[xxvii] Cooper, H. Et al., "Evidence of Eurasian Metal Alloys on the Alaskan Coast in Prehistory," *Journal of Archaeological Science* 74, p. 176-183, Oct 2016

[xxviii] Maschner H.D.G. et al., "An introduction to the biocomplexity of Sanak Island, western gulf of Alaska," *Pacific Science* 63: p. 673-709, 2009

[xxix] Barbeau, C.M., "The Aleutian Route of Migration into America," *Geographical Review* 35:3, p. 424-443, 1945

[xxx] Emmons, George, *The Tlingit Indians*, 1991

[xxxi] Lewis, Steve, "Kit'n'Caboodle Cave," *Alaska Caver* 14:6, 1994

[xxxii] Enrico, John, "Toward Proto-Na-Dene," *Anthropological Linguistics* 46(3): 229-302, 2004

[xxxiii] Emmons, George, *The Whale House of the Chilkat*, New York, Anthropological Papers of AMNH, 1916

[xxxiv] Menotti, Francesco, *Wetland Archeology and Beyond*, Oxford, Oxford University Press, 2012

[xxxv] Sackett, Russell, *The Chilkat Tlingit, A General Overview*, Fairbanks, UAS Press, 1979

[xxxvi] Keithahn, Edward, *Monuments in Cedar*, Seattle, Superior Publishing, 1963

[xxxvii] Duff, W., "Contributions of Marcus Barbeau to West Coast Ethnology," *Anthropologica* 6:1, p. 63-96, 1964

[xxxviii] Larson, Brendan, *The Proud Chilkat,* Juneau, Chilkat Press, 1977

[xxxix] Fladmark, K.R., *British Columbia Prehistory*, 1986

[xl] Kirk, R., *Wisdom of the Elders*, Vancouver, B.C. Provincial Museum, 1986

[xli] Cameron, Anne, *Daughters of Copper Woman*, Madeira Park BC, Harbour Publishing, 1981

HAWAII: HOMELAND

[xlii] Cameron, Anne, *Dzelarhons,* Madeira Park BC, Harbour Publishing, 1986

[xliii] Lee, P. and Willis, J., *Ho'opono*, Honolulu, Native Books, 1999

[xliv] Pukui, M.K. and Green, L., *Folk Tales of Hawaii*, Honolulu, Bishop Museum Press, 1995

[xlv] Masse, W. et al., "Exploring the nature of myth and its role in science," *Geological Society London Special Publications* 273, p. 9-28, 2007

[xlvi] Rouulier, C. et al., "Historical collections reveal patterns of sweet potato in Oceania," *Proceedings of Natl Academy of Sciences* 110 (6), p. 2205-2210, 5 Feb 2013

[xlvii] Wianecki, S., "Deep South," *Hana Hou* 20:4, 2017

[xlviii] Emory, K.P., W.J. Bonk and Y.H. Sinoto. 1959. *Hawaiian Archaeology: Fishhooks*, Special Publication 47. Honolulu, Bishop Museum, 1959

[xlix] Emory, K.P., and Simon, Y.H., "Age of Sites in the South Point Area, Ka'u, Hawaii," *Pacific Anthropological Records* 8, Honolulu, Bishop Museum, 1969

[l] Kelly, Marion, "Historical Background of the South Point Area, Ka'u, Hawaii," *Pacific Anthropological Records* No. 6, Honolulu, Bishop Museum, 1969

[li] Emory, K. P., and Sinoto, Y. H., ibid.

[lii] Hunt, T., and Olsen, R., "An Early Radiocarbon Chronology for the Hawaiian Islands," *Asian Perspective* Vol. 30, No. 1, pp. 147-161, 1991

[liii] Jensen, P.M., "Archaeological Data Recovery Program Lots 1, 2, 6, 17, 24, Waikoloa Beach Resort," Manuscript on file, Historic Sites Division, Department of Land and Natural Resources, Honolulu, 1989

[liv] Soehren, L.J., "Hawaii Excavations 1965. Manuscript on file, Library, Bishop Museum, Honolulu, 1966

[lv] Kirch, P., *Feathered Gods and Fishhooks: An Introduction to Hawaiian Archeology,* Honolulu, University of Hawaii Press, 1985

[lvi] Kwiatkowski, P.F., *Na Ki'i Pohaku*, Honolulu, University of Hawaii Press, 1991

[lvii] Kane, H.K., *Ancient Hawaii*, Captain Cook Hawaii, Kawainui Press, 1997

[lviii] Kirch, P., "Rethinking East Polynesian Prehistory," *Journal of the Polynesian Society* 95: 1, p. 9-40, 1985

[lix] Collerson, K.D. and Weisler, M.I., *Science* 317, p. 1907-1911, 2007

[lx] Skoglund, P. et al.,"Genomic insights into the peopling of the Southwest Pacific," *Nature* 538, p. 510-513, 27 Oct 2016

[lxi] Limderholm, et al., "A novel *MC1R* allele for black coat colour reveals the Polynesian ancestry and hybridization patterns of Hawaiian feral pigs," *Royal Society Open Science*, 7 Sep 2016

[lxii] Storey, A. et al., "Radiocarbon and DNA evidence for a pre-Columbian introduction of Polynesian chickens to Chile," *PNAS* 104: 25, p. 10335-10339 (2007)

[lxiii] Sharp, B., "Rock Inscriptions in Kauai, Hawaiian Islands," *Proceedings of Academy of Natural Science*, 1898, Philadelphia

[lxiv] McBride, L., *Petroglyphs in Hawaii*, Hilo, Petroglyph Press, 1969

[lxv] Filimoehala, D. et al., 'Hematite in Hawaii," *Hawaiian Archeology 14*, Honolulu, Society for Hawaiian Archeology, 2015

[lxvi] Pukui, M.K. and Green, L., *Folk Tales of Hawaii*, Honolulu, Bishop Museum Press, 1995

TAHITI: DISTANT LAND

[lxviii] Beaglehole, J.C., *The Life of Captain James Cook*, Stanford University Press, 1992

[lxix] Joesting, E., *Kauai: The Separate Kingdom*, Honolulu, University of Hawaii Press, 1984

[lxx] Emory, K., *Archeology of Nihoa and Necker Islands*, Honolulu, Bishop Museum Press, 1928

[lxxi] *Secret Instructions to Captain Cook*, 30 June 1768, National Archives of Australia

AOTEAROA/NEW ZEALAND

[lxxii] Wilson, Colin J. N., "The 26.5 ka Oruanui eruption, New Zealand," *Journal of Volcanology and Geothermal Research.* **112**: 133–174, 2001

[lxxiii] Orbell, Margaret, *The Illustrated Encyclopedia of Maori Myth and Legend*, Christchurch, Canterbury University Press, 1995

[lxxiv] Best, Elsdon, *The Maori Canoe*, Wellington, A.R. Shearer, 1925

[lxxv] Crowe, A., "New Zealand place names shared with the Hawaiian Archipelago," *Rapa Nui Journal* 27:1, May 2013

[lxxvi] Mills, C. and Parke, T., "Dogs of Rarotonga," *Discover* 25 Jun 2004

[lxxvii] Rogers D. S.& Ehrlich P. R, "Natural selection and cultural rates of change," *Proc. Natl Acad. Sci.* **105**, 3416–3420. 2008

[lxxviii] Rogers, D. et al., "Inferring population histories using cultural data, " *Proceedings of Royal Society B* 276:1674 (2009)

[lxxix] Smith, S.P., *Hawai'iki, the original home of the Maori*, Melbourne, Whitcombe and Tombs, 1904

[lxxx] Wood, J.R. Et al., "Origin and timing of New Zealand's earliest domestic chickens…" *Royal Society Open Source,* 3 Aug 2016

[lxxxi] Smith, P., Hawaiki: the whence of the Maori with a sketch of Polynesian history, Whitcombe & Tombs, 1898

[lxxxii] Hitchcock, G., "The Final Fate of the La Pérouse Expedition?..." *Journal of Pacific History* 52: 2 (2017)

[lxxxiii][lxxxiii] Vancouver, G., *A Voyage of Discovery to the North Pacific Ocean and Round the World in the Years 1790-95,* London, 1798

[lxxxiv] Voss, J.C., *The Venturesome Voyages of Captain Voss*, New York, Dodd, Mead & Co., 1926

[lxxxv] Lowman Carey, B., *Bijaboji: North to Alaska by Oar,* Madeira Park BC, Harbour Publishing, 2004

[lxxxvi] Smith, S.P., *Hawai'iki the whence of the Maori,* Wellington, Whitcombe & Tombes, 1898

I'A: GALAXY

[lxxxvii] Anglada-Escude, G. et al., "A terrestrial planet candidate in a temperate orbit around Proxima Centauri," *Nature* **536**, p. 437–440 (2016)

[lxxxviii] Benner, S., "Planets, Minerals, and Life's Origin," *Goldschmidt 2013 Conference Abstracts,* Florence (2013) https://phys.org/news/2013-08-martians-theory-life-mars.html

[lxxxix] Sharov, A., and Gordon, R., "Life Before Earth," arxiv.org/abs/1304.3381

About the Author

LOUISE RIOFRIO is educated in physics and astronomy. Since 2008 she has been working as a Scientist at NASA Johnson Space Center in Houston. While studying the Moon, she performed experiments with Apollo lunar samples. She is known worldwide for predicting and measuring a change in the Speed of Light. She has been invited to speak before scientific conferences worldwide. She has also worked as a Naturalist in Alaska, helping to rescue Bald Eagles. Louise Riofrio is also author of THE SPEED OF LIGHT, a popular science book.

Cover photo (top) courtesy Mira
Cover photo (bottom) courtesy Paul Bica
Haida Gwai'i map courtesy Kelsi

Made in the USA
Middletown, DE
25 June 2021